TOOLS
FOR
Daily Inspirations
LIFE

TOOLS FOR LIFE

FOR
LIFE

Daily Inspirations

DR. JAMES COYLE

iUniverse®

TOOLS FOR LIFE
DAILY INSPIRATIONS

All scriptures are taken from the Holy Bible, New International Version®. NIV®. Copyright © 1973, 1978, 1984 by International Bible Society. Used by permission of Zondervan. All rights reserved. [Biblica]

iUniverse books may be ordered through booksellers or by contacting:

iUniverse
1663 Liberty Drive
Bloomington, IN 47403
www.iuniverse.com
1-800-Authors (1-800-288-4677)

ISBN: 978-1-5320-3379-7 (sc)
ISBN: 978-1-5320-3381-0 (hc)
ISBN: 978-1-5320-3380-3 (e)

Library of Congress Control Number: 2017918560

Print information available on the last page.

iUniverse rev. date: 01/18/2018

CONTENTS

FOREWORD

Dr. James Coyle is continuing to live his life mission of helping people get to a better place. *Tools for Life* was conceived from a lifetime of experience of assisting people through difficult circumstances and seasons. In his first book, *GPS: Your Guide through Personal Storms*, Dr. Coyle offered a guide for people to navigate through the different storms of life. *Tools for Life* is a collection of 365 daily inspirational readings focused on providing encouragement and motivation for the day-to-day challenges of life. The stories are based on personal and professional experiences. Dr. Coyle's background as a counselor, professor, pastor, first responder, and human relations director has fueled him to write these short daily stories. The writings follow a theme of providing daily tools and resources for everyday decisions and choices for men and women, as well as teenagers. The stories are not in any specific order and can be read year after year to provide direction and reassurance in the struggles and victories throughout life. There are seasonal reflections throughout the book, along with acknowledgments of some holidays that have the same date every year. The dates mentioned are there for the purpose of helping you keep a daily record of readings and to offer a place to return if you miss a day. The readings can be handed down to generations of family and friends and can influence them over lifetimes. *Tools for Life* is a resource that will provide insightful guidance and comforting care to its readers. The book is designed to be picked up on any day throughout the year. Enjoy its content and share its visions, understandings, and perceptions with people you care about.
Dr. Lisa Coyle, PhD, licensed school counselor

HAPPY NEW "OPPORTUNITY" YEAR

We spend too much time focused on the rearview mirror. The might-have-been, the should-have-been, and the could-have-been are all behind us. The things behind us have helped pave the way for the things that are ahead of us. The more we replay yesterday, the more distracted we are today. As modern-day philosopher Maria Robinson is quoted as saying, "Nobody can go back and start a new beginning, but anyone can start today and make a new ending." As we march into the New Year, let's make this a year of opportunities. Opportunities don't wait for anyone. They come from many directions and in many forms. One thing for certain is that opportunities are very clear and vivid when we miss them. We must be in the present to grasp them. That is why we have to focus on the present and not the past. We can't afford to miss out on opportunities. Look for them and seize them. "Jesus said, 'No procrastination. No backward looks. You can't put God's kingdom off till tomorrow. Seize the day'" (Luke 9:62). Here is the beauty of a caught opportunity: it opens the door for others. They will piggyback on each other. The people influenced by our seized opportunities will then have their own opportunities to grasp. Every caught opportunity casts seeds of life onto fertile ground. Don't miss out on opportunities—look for them and grab them. Happy New Opportunity Year.

NEW YEAR OPPORTUNITY

Amid the global tragedies that have blanketed a country in sadness and grief, there is hope for a better year if we can embrace an opportunity to change. Healthy change is a direct result of a changed attitude and behavior. We have an undisciplined world that is running rampant with fuel from fear, anger, and depression. The only way to bridle an effective change is *discipline.* Discipline is doing the things you know you should do even when you don't feel like doing them. Discipline is the glue between words and accomplishments. Discipline is bringing your state of being to obedience of authority (disciple).

- Be intentional about doing the things you know you should do but don't feel like doing.
- Use the scriptures to guide you.
- Discipline (disciple) yourself.
- Put your victory trophies on the mantel of your heart, and give God the glory.

HIGH SCHOOL RESPONDS—PART ONE

This is a statement that was read over the public-announcement system at a football game at a high school in Tennessee: "It has always been the custom here to say a prayer and play the national anthem to honor God and country. Due to a ruling by the Supreme Court, I am told that saying a prayer is a violation of federal case law. As I understand the law at this time, I can use this public facility to approve of sexual differences and call it an alternative lifestyle, and if someone is offended, that's okay. I can use it to condone sexual promiscuity by dispensing condoms and calling it safe sex. If someone is offended, that's okay. I can even use this public facility to present the merits of abortion as a viable means of birth control. If someone is offended, no problem. I can designate a school day as Earth Day and involve students in activities to worship religiously and praise the goddess 'Mother Earth' and call it ecology. I can use literature, videos, and presentations in the classroom that depict people with strong, traditional convictions as 'simple minded' and 'ignorant' and call it enlightenment. However, if anyone uses this facility to honor God and to ask Him to *bless* this event with safety and good sportsmanship, then federal case law is violated."

HIGH SCHOOL RESPONDS—PART TWO

The statement continued. "This appears to be inconsistent at best and at worst very judgmental. Apparently, we are to be tolerant of everything and anyone, except God and His commandments. Nevertheless, as a school principal, I frequently ask staff and students to abide by rules with which they do not necessarily agree. For me to do otherwise would be inconsistent at best and at worst hypocritical … I suffer from that affliction enough unintentionally. I certainly do not need to add an intentional transgression. For this reason, I shall 'render unto Caesar that which is Caesar's' and refrain from praying at this time. However, if you feel inspired to honor, praise, and thank God and ask Him, in the name of Jesus, to bless this event, please feel free to do so. As far as I know, that's not against the law—yet." One by one, the people in the stands bowed their heads, held hands with one another, and began to pray. They prayed in the stands. They prayed in the team huddles. They prayed at the concession stand, and they prayed in the announcer's box! The only place they didn't pray was in the Supreme Court of the United States of America—the seat of "justice" in the "one nation, under *God*." Somehow, people at a high school in Tennessee remembered what so many have forgotten. We are given the freedom *of* religion, not the freedom *from* religion. Thank you to our forefathers!

FIVE-MINUTE STRESS BUSTERS

If we allow it, stress can steal our time, capture our thoughts, and put a wet blanket on a good day. By the time we put our heads on our pillows, we are wound as tight as a yo-yo. Trying to sleep regularly is almost impossible. Then, we wake up the next morning and start the hamster wheel all over again. Here are some ways to get around the stressors throughout the day. Apply these five-minute stress busters and get back the life that you so deserve.

- Take a five-minute stress-release walk outdoors Contact with a fresh environment is especially beneficial.
- Spend five minutes listening to a recording featuring your favorite comedian.
- Take a five-minute nap after lunch; the alarm on your cell phone is wonderful.
- Take five minutes visualizing yourself relaxing at your favorite vacation spot.
- Take five minutes for a gentle neck roll and shoulder massage.

BOOT CAMP—PART ONE

No matter what you hear, where you turn, or what you watch, the message is loud and clear: the world is in a mess. The Bible is very clear on predicting the times we are in and the times to come. The picture the world is painting for tomorrow isn't pretty, but the portrait of God is being hand-painted for our victory. We need to equip ourselves and train our kids for the battle we are in right now and the battle we are facing tomorrow. Here are a few things we should know and do: know the battleground, prepare yourself, know your enemy, use the Word, fight, and rest at the end of the day. "For our struggle is not against flesh and blood, but against the rulers, against the authorities, against the powers of this dark world and against the spiritual forces of evil in the heavenly realms" (Eph. 6:12). We will learn how to use our heads, our hearts, and our hands to walk forward in the fight of our lives. We will be encouraged as we face circumstances where we will need one another and the Holy Spirit to keep moving forward in the face of battle.

BOOT CAMP—PART TWO: THE BELT OF TRUTH AND BREASTPLATE OF RIGHTEOUSNESS

We are being equipped and trained to use the armor of God in our life battle against the enemy. The first part of our armor is the belt of truth securely strapped around our core (waist). The core is the vital foundation of all of the body's movement. It gives us a strong, firm spine and stability in facing spiritual battles. Knowing the truth is the foundation of our stance with God. "Jesus said, 'I am the way, the truth, and the life' (John 14:6). "You will know the truth and the truth will set you free," (John 8:32). The next piece of armor is the breastplate of righteousness. It protects our vital organs, which include the heart, lungs, kidneys, and other body parts. Keeping the heart protected is critical in facing our enemy. The breastplate protects us in doing the right thing by loving God with all our heart. The first two pieces of armor, the belt of truth and the breastplate of righteousness, are essential in equipping us to fight in the war given to us through the victory at the cross. Next, we will continue to put on the armor of God.

BOOT CAMP—PART THREE: LEGS AND HEAD

We continue to put on our spiritual armor in recognizing that our battles are not against flesh and blood but against spirits of evil that pollute our heads, hearts, and hands. We talked about securing our core with the belt of truth and protecting our vital organs with the breastplate of righteousness. Today, we focus on getting our feet fitted with the readiness that comes from the gospel of peace and the helmet of salvation. The warrior's legs are covered from the knees to the feet, and the feet are protected by one- to three-inch spikes at the bottom of the soles to allow the soldier to be firmly planted or to navigate difficult terrain. The helmet is the last piece of body armor we put on before going to battle. The head is most vulnerable to injury, and the helmet protects us and identifies us as to what team we belong. It also helps insulate the body from inclement weather. With our core supported, our vital organs protected, and our legs and feet firmly planted, we have the helmet of salvation to protect our thoughts from contamination of evil. We also have our identity with the big letter J in our faith. And we have an insulation of the Holy Spirit to help control our emotions and mental dysfunctions associated with evil.

BOOT CAMP—PART FOUR: SHIELD AND SWORD

Today we finish putting on the armor of God in our battle against the principalities of this dark world. As we have discussed, it is vitally important to have our heads, hearts, and hands all on the same page, especially in the face of battle. The helmet of salvation protects our heads in the battle of our thoughts. It gives us our identity on God's team and insulates us from internal conflict. Our hearts and vital organs are protected by the breastplate of righteousness (doing the right thing), and our legs and feet are protected as we stand firm against the attacks of evil with the gospel of peace. Our hands are used to hold the shield of faith and the sword of the Spirit, which is the Word of God. In one hand, the shield gives us protection from the fiery arrows of evil while we also hold on to something that is greater than what we see, our faith. The other hand is holding the sword (the Word of God) that is used defensively to have divine power over evil and offensively to carve the path God has prepared for us. So our heads are protected in the battle in our minds, our hearts are protected from the deceit of evil, and our hands are used purposefully for the fulfillment of God's plan for our lives. Gear up for the battle of life.

LEARNING TO LIVE FOR OTHERS

Though we may not see it in the present, all the things we are going through have a purpose in our lives. The sandpaper burns of our experiences will help mold us and smooth us out to benefit others. People are driven by passions from something they have seen, felt, heard, or done. If people have been abused spiritually, physically, or emotionally and are committed to a healing process, they are often led to assist others who are experiencing similar pain, suffering, or affliction. One of the best ways we can heal is to give back. I survived an attempted suicide in 1977. The pain I experienced as a nineteen-year-old was overwhelming, and I thought the only escape was to end my life. As a result, my survival has led me to assist others who are contemplating suicide and those who are survivors of suicide. Our pain and suffering can be used to help others if we let them. Jesus led by example and has challenged us to take up our cross. Our purpose can be fulfilled when our lives benefit others. Life is about learning to live for others.

AM I A BLESSING OR A CURSE?

In a recent Little League baseball game, I watched the demise of a team that had an eight-run lead with two innings left to play in a championship game. The coaches started tearing down the players and challenging them as if they were losing. Old tapes were replayed of previous failings, and the morale and attitude of the team sank as if in quicksand as the game was lost in the bottom of the last inning. I am humbled to say that, as a coach of that team, I set the table with what was put on our plates. Our words have power to build up or tear down. "Out of the same mouth comes blessing and cursing" (James 3:10). I realize that I may not have had an impact on the results of the game, but I did have an impact on the kids. The lesson I learned was to purpose in my heart to say a blessing rather than a curse. If I can recapture the moment to instruct again, I will teach a different way to communicate. "When you talk, don't say anything bad. But say the good things that people need—whatever will help them grow stronger. Then what you say will be a blessing to those who hear you" (Eph. 4:29).

BEND A KNEE—
DON'T POINT A FINGER

We have control over two particular parts of our bodies that we can either bend or straighten out—the knee and the pointer finger. The reason I am focusing on these two is because the knee and the pointer finger have the power to change many outcomes in life if we can learn to use them properly. By pointing a finger, we are not accepting responsibility but placing the blame on someone or something else. Blame-shifting abusers have difficulty taking responsibility for problems and taking ownership for emotions. They go as far as necessary to attribute blame for their circumstances to anyone else but themselves. However, a bent knee puts one in a positon of acceptance and humility. Bending a knee sends a message of responsibility and restoration. We automatically lower ourselves in comparison to other people, which allows us to look up rather than look down. Pointing a finger puts us up on a stepladder, looking and pointing down. Paul hit the nail on the head when he said: "Do nothing out of selfish ambition or vain conceit. Rather, in humility value others above yourselves" (Phil. 2:3). Practice bending the knee and the finger. The sooner we learn to bend a knee and not point a finger, the sooner we will be part of the solution and not the problem.

THREE-DAY RULE

While I was having lunch with a dear friend, he inspired me with his approach to handling tough events, which he called the three-day rule. It went as follows.

- **Day one:** This is the day to catch your breath after getting the wind knocked out of you. Ask for God's guidance as you begin to sort it out. It could come from the Bible, signs, other people, or a combination of things to help comfort you.
- **Day two:** This is the day to look at how and why the situation happened. If it was something that could have been prevented, what can you learn from it and how can you make things better? If it was outside of your control, how can you use it to make yourself a better person?
- **Day three:** This is the day to move on and put what happened behind you so it doesn't trip you as you move toward what lies ahead. Put it on the shelf and keep it there to remind of where you came from.

Thank you, Ralph, for your words of wisdom.

A TOUCH IN THE DARKEST HOUR

Every one of us will personally experience or know someone who has been in his or her darkest hour. This is the place with no light at the end of the tunnel. We as a whole lost someone recently, Robin Williams, who suffered in his darkest hour. Humans have labeled a multitude of mental health disorders that have roots in depression. Labels validate people's pain and give them a reason to sink lower in the name of their diagnosis. Pharmaceutical companies are gaining millions of dollars from various prescriptions in attempts to bring comfort in people's darkest hour. The critical thing that must take place for survival is the removal of the victim label, replacing it with a label of victor. The scriptures talk of resources from heaven in the midst of a paralyzed state of mind. When Peter was facing his darkest hour, on the eve of his execution, "the church was earnestly praying." Prayer behind the scenes is a source of unknown spiritual strength. Twice, when Jesus was in His darkest hour, an angel touched Him and gave Him strength to move forward in his immobile state. The scriptures are full of examples of angels providing strength when the tunnel is dark. When we get our senses and strength back, our faith in Christ allows us to live and move forward. Whether we are in our earthly body suit or heavenly body suit, we live in eternity through Christ.

DOING THE RIGHT THING

I read a story that captured my heart. It involves a nineteen-year-old college basketball player with inoperable brain cancer. The National Collegiate Athletic Association gave special permission for two colleges to begin play before the normal starting date so that she could play. Doing the right thing filled an arena, a state, a nation, and a world with hope and purpose. The cloud of an act of kindness rains and soaks those who are fortunate enough to be under it. This is an example of cross-pollinating among corporate America, the bureaucracy of higher educational institutions, the council of medical doctors, and the will and desire of a young, determined athlete. When we come together to do the right thing, barriers become bridges and bridges become paths to walk and live each day, as it is meant to be. Doing the right thing gives us a "Get off the hamster wheel free" card. This nineteen-year-old girl turned a death sentence into a life lesson: that we need to live each day, as it is our beginning, not our end.

B3: THE PROFILE OF A WARRIOR

Kingdom Warriors Wanted: Join us as we connect the passion of our hearts with the skillfulness of our hands in helping people find hope and purpose with their lives. Let's unwrap the fiber of a kingdom warrior. This profile was designed by and lived out through the life of Jesus. There are three Bs that make up a kingdom warrior. The first B is *broken,* a state of being in which only God can renew us. This is when the wind is out of our sails and we must rely on something we don't have. "My sacrifice, O God, is a broken spirit; a broken and contrite heart you, God, will not despise" (Ps. 51:17). The second B is blessing, an open window for God to bring us hope and purpose. Jesus covered a multitude of blessings as recorded in Matthew 5, known as the Beatitudes. The third B is *benefit*, a state of being in which our lives are being used to benefit others. "If anyone speaks, they should do so as one who speaks the very words of God. If anyone serves, they should do so with the strength God provides" (1 Peter 4:11). Every kingdom warrior is broken, blessed, and used to benefit others. If you want to be a warrior, follow the path that was prepared for you.

COMMUNICATION: MANY THINGS GET IN THE WAY—PART ONE

So many things get in the way in the communication process. Whether we are sending or receiving a message, the same filters and barriers exist. These are speed bumps and hurdles in the perception of the message. We will discuss many of these obstacles so that we can become aware of the misrepresentations and distortions that can take place.

- **Nonverbal messages:** Studies have shown that nonverbal messaging accounts for 93 percent of communication. Nonverbal communications are messages without words. We live in a world that relies on social media to communicate. People make relational commitments, companies make corporate decisions, and countries react to information that is communicated through social media. Facial expressions, eye contact, body gestures, and personal space are critical in the interpretation of messages.
- **Facial expressions:** Facial expressions are some of the best indicators of another person's emotions and feelings. Understanding facial expressions can help us in the communication process. Several universal emotions are communicated through facial expressions: happiness, sadness, contempt, surprise, disgust, anger, and fear.
- **Body gestures:** Body gestures are a sure way to convey a reaction to a message. Depending on the culture and

environment, body gestures project a message that could easily be misunderstood. Even hand gestures have different meanings in different cultures, such as the okay sign, the rubbing of the thumb and forefingers, and thumbs-up.

COMMUNICATION: MANY THINGS GET IN THE WAY—PART TWO

Even if we communicate clearly when speaking verbally, other forms of communication may enhance or interfere with our messages. Below are some examples of nonverbal forms of communication.

- **Eye contact:** Our eyes communicate more information than any other part of our bodies. Depending on the culture, people will generally evaluate messages that are being communicated through the eyes. People who have a prolonged and direct stare could be perceived as being threatening, dangerous, or unsafe. People who don't look others in the eye can be perceived as having no confidence, being guilty, or feeling ashamed. It is good to have eye contact at least 60 percent of the time in North America. In some other countries, eye contact could be perceived as disrespectful.
- **Personal space:** People use the space around them in communicating a message. If people are too close, they may feel uncomfortable. If they are too far apart, they may also feel uncomfortable. Eighteen inches around a person's body is considered intimate space.
- **Emotions:** Strong emotions can interfere with what is being communicated in a message. Detaching yourself from another's emotions can be challenging, as can trying to manage your own. Messages can be better understood if we can separate ourselves from emotions during the communication process.

COMMUNICATION: MANY THINGS GET IN THE WAY—PART THREE

Whether receiving or sending messages there are constant obstacles and hurdles in the perception and intent of what's being communicated.

- **Role expectations:** Our expectations of how people should act or respond because of their positions or titles can affect the communication process. Some people may use their roles to alter the way they relate to others by positioning themselves higher than others because of a need for power. Others may have a difficult time adjusting or accepting a new position that changes the former way of communication.
- **The roles of men and women:** Gender-specific roles begin to take shape during early childhood and continue through adult life. Depending on the culture, boys and girls and men and women are expected to communicate a certain way. Men are generally more competitive and will communicate by using an upper hand to negotiate. Women are generally more support-oriented and social in their peacemaking role.
- **Semantics:** The same word can have multiple meanings. These words appear in our language often, especially in the younger generations. The words *cool* and *hip* have different meanings depending on their usage in conversation. Thousands of slang words can influence the communication process.

GET OFF THE BENCH

Life is going by at a hectic pace. You were designed and created for something much more than making a living. The time for you to stand up is now. The poet William Arthur Ward wrote,

> I will do more than belong: I will participate.
> I will do more than care: I will help.
> I will do more than believe: I will practice.
> I will do more than be fair: I will be kind.
> I will do more than forgive: I will forget.
> I will do more than dream: I will work.
> I will do more than teach: I will inspire.
> I will do more than learn: I will enrich.
> I will do more than give: I will serve.
> I will do more than live: I will grow.
> I will do more than suffer: I will triumph.

You must believe in God, believe in yourself, and have the faith to do what you are called to do. It's time to get off the bench.

OUR TRUE REWARD IS WAITING

The story is told of an elderly missionary couple who were returning home on a ship after many years of sacrificial service in Africa. On the same ship was Theodore Roosevelt, who had just completed a highly successful big game hunt. As the ship docked in New York Harbor, thousands of well-wishers and dozens of reporters lined the pier to welcome Roosevelt home. But not a single person was there to welcome the missionaries. As the couple rode to a hotel in a taxi, the man complained to his wife, "It just doesn't seem right. We give forty years of our lives to Jesus Christ to win souls in Africa, and nobody knows or cares when we return. Yet the president goes over there for a few weeks to kill some animals and the whole world takes notice." But as they prayed together that night before retiring, the Lord seemed to say to them, *Do you know why you haven't received your reward yet? It is because you are not home yet.* It's so easy to get swept into earthly rewards when our true reward is waiting.

NO MORE BLAME GAME

I once saw an old *Dennis the Menace* cartoon in which Dennis was being disciplined and sitting on his rocking chair in the corner of a room. The caption read, "I'm sitting down on the outside, but I'm still standing up on the inside." What a great depiction of our natural tendency to not accept responsibility. I have competitive teenage twins who are constantly at each other and holding the other responsible for any wrongdoing or coming up with an excuse. One of the hardest lessons in life to teach our kids is taking responsibility for wrong behavior. What's even more difficult is leading by example. A major contributor to maturing is taking responsibility no matter what age we are. We start as infants with no responsibility. Everything is done for us. As we progress through the various stages of childhood, we take on more and more responsibility. We learn to tie our own shoes, clean our own rooms, and turn in our own homework. We learn that there are rewards for being responsible and consequences for not being responsible. In many ways, the difference between a child and an adult is one's willingness to take personal responsibility for one's actions. As Paul said, "When I became a man, I put the ways of childhood behind me" (1 Corin. 13:11). No more blame game.

WHAT'S THE BEST?

Are you ever stuck or torn about a decision and don't know the right one to make? The average person makes thirty-five thousand choices a day. The majority of our choices are a result of previous choices, so the tough part is making the right choice. How do I make the *best* choice? Paul wrote, "And this is my prayer: that your love may abound more and more in knowledge and depth of insight, so that you may be able to discern what is best and may be pure and blameless" (Phil. 1:9–10). If we are rooted and motivated in love and can wrap our minds around knowledge and insight, we will have the tools needed to make the right choice. The result of the best choice is knowing that we have done our best and can rest in it.

WANTED: KINGDOM WARRIORS

During the "Heroic Age of Exploration," Sir Ernest Shackleton coordinated the British Imperial Trans-Antarctic Expedition with the goal of accomplishing the first crossing of the Antarctic continent, a feat considered to be the last great polar journey. His first attempt to recruit his crew failed miserably. He reworded his recruitment notice to say, "Men wanted for hazardous journey. Small wages. Bitter cold. Long months of complete darkness. Constant danger. Safe return doubtful. Honor and recognition in case of success." In December 1914, Shackleton set sail with his twenty-seven-man crew. Although they withstood the most incredible hardship and privation, not one of the twenty-eight men was lost.

Wanted: Kingdom Warriors—Join me as I connect the passion of my heart with the skillfulness of my hands in helping people find hope and purpose in their kingdom lives.

THE PERFECT DAY

Have you ever wondered what a perfect day looks like? Think about it—twenty-four hours to make a difference in your life and in the lives of others. Scriptures teach us to live one day at a time. What does that look like? We have three functions of our being: **h**eart, **h**ands, and **h**ead. When we roll independently with one or two of these functions, our day is full of pot(ty) holes. When all three work and stay together, we will have the perfect day. There is a glue that binds all three together, and that is the Word of God. Once all three of the Hs are in line with heavenly mortar—the Word of God—there is divine direction with kingdom purpose. God's Word teaches us how to live a holy daily life and how to be fruitful witnesses to others under the rising and setting of the *Son*. "So commit yourselves whole*heart*edly to these words of mine. Tie them to your *hands* and wear them on your fore*head* as reminders. Teach them to your children when you're sitting in your home and when you are on the road, and when you go to bed, and when you are getting up. Write them on the doorposts of your house and on your gates" (Deuteronomy 11:18-20). So, if you want a perfect day, start with your HHH under the authority of the Word. Stay connected in your home, car, job, and back home again. Mark your turf, rest, and do it all over tomorrow.

STAY
BETWEEN THE LINES

So many things in life make us swerve outside the lines of our emotional, spiritual, and physical being. There are certain guidelines for us to follow that will keep us out of the ditch and prevent us from crossing the double yellow lines. If you want to know where you are going and if you are in your lane, look at your habits. Your habits determine your direction. The victory in staying in your lane is doing the right thing day after day. If you can do that, you will protect your lane and help prevent accidents from any accidents.

- Don't lose your character while you are trying to build your reputation. Character is what God knows about you. Reputation is what people think they know about you.
- Don't sacrifice your family for your career. You may win the admiration of those who don't matter while losing the love of those who do.
- Don't sacrifice your relationship with God for the relationships of this world. Your relationship with God will allow you to ascend while the relationships with the world will cause you to descend.

"Your word is a lamp to my feet and a light to my path" (Ps. 119:105). Stay between the lines.

FRUIT INSPECTION

On a long desert stretch of I-15 between Las Vegas and Los Angeles lies an agriculture inspection station on the California border. Each car must go through the security station as a law forbids the transfer of fruit into California to keep the California fruit from being contaminated. Likewise, there is a heavenly border patrolled by the Holy Spirit to keep heaven's fruit protected. These nine fruits are identified in Galatians 5:22–23: "The Holy Spirit produces this kind of fruit in our lives: love, joy, peace, patience, kindness, goodness, faithfulness, gentleness, and self-control." Now is a great time to inspect the fruit in your life. The first step is to believe and receive. *Faith* means believing something, trusting in something, and depending on something. Faithfulness is living a certain way because you believe in that "something." Fruit is the result of the way you live. Get on the right side of the border and protect your fruit with the way you live: *love, joy, peace, patience, kindness, goodness, faithfulness, gentleness, and self-control.* Come, Holy Spirit, and produce these fruits while protecting them and us from the contaminants of life.

LIFE IN GOD'S GARDEN

"The LORD God planted a garden eastward in Eden, and there He put the man whom He had formed" (Gen. 2:8).

- **Be prepared:** There is a process of preparation God takes us through in order to make us what we need to be.
- **Be planted:** Seeds are planted beyond human view so that they may germinate and eventually produce fruit.
- **Be placed:** God took man and placed him in the garden.
- **Be pruned:** Now you have to work at it. Stop looking for gardens that are already pruned. You must go through your own struggles and shed your own tears.
- **Be prosperous:** Learn to prosper in the fruits of the kingdom and not the fruits of the world.

"But the fruit of the Spirit is love, joy, peace, patience, kindness, goodness, faithfulness, gentleness and self-control" (Gal. 5:22–23). The fruits of the Spirit are a good indication of how we are doing in God's garden.

UNDERSTANDING TRAUMA: PHYSICALLY, EMOTIONALLY, AND SPIRITUALLY—PART ONE

All of us have either experienced or know someone who has experienced trauma. It is a result of a horrible loss or an extreme difficulty. Trauma is a perceived element of actual or threatened death or serious injury to oneself or others. Most people recover from traumatic events without long-lasting problems. If the event or circumstance continues to cause sleepless nights and ruminating thoughts, professional help may be needed. Some factors that can increase trauma are the proximity to the event or circumstance, the duration of exposure to the event or circumstance, and the severity of the event or circumstance. Trauma can be divided into two categories that can affect our physical, emotional, and spiritual beings. The first is invasive trauma, the kind that creates damage. The second is desertion trauma—the result of something that *didn't* happen to a person, such as abandonment and feeling deserted. This is difficult to recognize because people may not know what they are missing if they never had it. Understanding trauma is critical to the healing process of being able to grow forward despite what has happened. Let's explore the different aspects of invasive and desertion trauma.

UNDERSTANDING TRAUMA: PHYSICALLY, EMOTIONALLY, AND SPIRITUALLY—PART TWO

Trauma can influence our decisions as we go through life. Being aware of trauma and where it comes from is helpful in our abilities to continue to survive and grow. Invasive trauma is a result of something that has happened to us. Physically, invasive trauma occurs when there is abuse or an unknown outside elements, such as a hurricane, fire, earthquake, tornado, or any other catastrophic event. This form of trauma can cause permanent physical damage. Emotionally, invasive trauma occurs when people feel blamed, criticized, or shamed. This can be both verbal and nonverbal. People also can be labeled and live under the scrutiny of that label. Emotional scars from invasive trauma can be permanent if not dealt with. Spiritually, invasive trauma takes place when rigid, fear-based religious training results in feelings of unworthiness and shame. Desertion trauma is a result of something that hasn't happened to us. Physically, desertion trauma happens when our basic needs for food, shelter, and clothing aren't met. Another form is lack of touch. Emotionally, desertion trauma results in loneliness and occurs when love, nurture, care, and affirmations aren't present. Spiritually, desertion trauma manifests when clergy or religious authorities cause profound damage, such as by passing on unhealthy spiritual teachings.

IT'S OKAY
TO BE DIFFERENT

Have you wondered why it is so easy to talk to some people and so difficult to talk to others? Have you ever caught yourself wanting to disappear from a room when someone pushes your exit button? It is so important for us to realize that people have different communication styles that might rub us the wrong way. Once I accept that not everyone is like me, my world gets a little bigger. Here are some different communication styles:

- *Leave me alone* **style:** Usually quiet, alone, and introverted
- *Take charge* **style**: Frank, assertive, and controlling
- *You make the choice* **style**: Not attention seeking, patient, and passive
- *It's all about me* **style**: Likes the limelight, spontaneous, and persuasive

I'M TIRED—PART ONE

Have you ever been at a place in your career or your marriage where you were tired? You become fatigued to the point that you lose hope and direction, causing you to doubt whether what you're doing is really making a difference. If your life commitment and service are about helping people, you are highly susceptible to facing fatigue, burnout, exhaustion, and apathy. You are overtired physically, spiritually, and emotionally. The snowball is rolling down the hill, and you see a crash coming at the bottom. The things you do for other people have affected the values that you have for yourself. Somehow, the demands of your service in helping others have compromised the values of your family or significant relationships. It becomes very difficult to separate your work life from your home life. I want to offer some tools for you to try to put fuel back in your tank and help you get the meaningful rest that your pillow is patiently waiting to provide. Stressors can be overwhelming. If we can walk beside the stressors and take their power away, we can recapture a life that is being stolen right under our watch.

I'M TIRED—PART TWO

Self-care is critical in trying to rebound from an exhausting season. The following tools are to help in guiding you and helping you to sustain hope, desire, passion, and fuel to keep going without crashing at the bottom of the hill.

- Understand and accept that you are tired and in trouble. Find ways to check your oil and make sure you have fuel in your tank. There are many resources for you to consider. "Ask and it will be given to you; seek and you will find; knock and the door will be opened to you. For everyone who asks receives; the one who seeks finds; and to the one who knocks, the door will be opened" (Matt. 7:7–8)
- Create space and time for being quiet and alone. Johnny Carson conducted an interview with a woman who should have been drained and unable to keep moving forward in her life. Her name was Mother Teresa. She was the caregiver of all caregivers. She said the only way she survived each day was to create a quiet place for her and God. That was her fuel. She would spend four hours a day in her quiet place. That is almost inconceivable. Start small with ten minutes and add time as you can.

I'M TIRED—PART THREE

I continue in assisting you in understanding the importance of self-care. Self-care is of the utmost importance in managing the stressors that used to control you. These tools are to help you sustain hope, desire, passion, and fuel to keep going without crashing into a ditch.

- Talk to someone you trust and in whom you can confide. Find a person who can understand how you feel and walk beside you. Keep in mind the words of Friedrich Nietzsche: "There will be but few people who, when at a loss for topics of conversation, will not reveal the more secret affairs of their friends."

- Commit to a lifestyle that will help sustain you. Healthy eating habits have tremendous benefits to your physical being as well as your mental being. Good food recharges a depleting body. Regular exercise will reduce stress and reenergize you for time with family and friends.

- Have an intentional conversation with someone about something meaningful. Also, ask God for a divine appointment. Commit to having two conversations in your day—one you can control and one you can't. You will find the conversations that you don't control will fill you up. When you are available, God will use you. Be available.

I'M TIRED—PART FOUR

The final two tools to discuss and apply in your weary life are very important to putting air back in your tires. They are also meant to help you sustain hope, desire, passion, and fuel to keep going. This is like putting the oxygen mask on your face before you can help someone else with theirs. Your lungs will not survive if you don't fill them before trying to fill someone else's.

- Simplify your life by taking steps to do less, ask for help, and stop being all things to all people. Talk to the one or ones who are suffering with you and develop some healthy boundaries together. Start focusing on balancing your relationships rather than the reasons you can't. A commitment to agree upon boundaries will bring hope back into a hopeless situation. You will see light at the end of a very dark tunnel and realize that you are not alone.

- Get help! If you are overwhelmed to the point of throwing in the towel, get some help. If the stressors have led to depression, anxiety, substance abuse, shopping, TV, overeating, and other forms of escape, it's time to get some professional help. Outside help can assist you with monitoring your thoughts, emotions, and behaviors. Professional assistance can help change a thought such as *I can do this by myself* to *I don't have to do this by myself.*

FLAMING ARROWS

I grew up watching old Westerns. One of the common scenes involved a covered wagon isolated in the middle of an open field. The wagon was encircled by the enemy, which presented an all-out attack with flaming arrows. Every day we wake up, we are faced with flaming arrows coming from all around us. They represent an attack on us and can come out of nowhere without any warning. They can also represent events and circumstances that we are aware of and must face. One of the most difficult responses to flaming arrows to learn is to defend from the inside of our core being and not be controlled by the heat of the outside elements. Don't look at what's happening around you; look at what's happening within you. This sounds like great advice, but the difficulty is in trying to apply it. I must slow down and gather myself during the battle. If I have the chance to prepare for something I am about to face, my best chance to survive is to rely on my inner being. If I am to survive a surprise attack, I must also rely on my inner being. I must learn to hold on to and rely on my core values.

LET IT GROW

This is a great time of year if you like watching the finals of sporting events. Whether it is Triple Crown horse racing, basketball, hockey, baseball, football, or another type of sport, there are always those who don't win. the 149th Belmont Stakes race captured the hearts of many who wanted so badly to see a Triple Crown winner. Here is one of the most important lessons in life: "All athletes are disciplined in their training. They do it to win a prize that will fade away, but we do it for an eternal prize. So I run with purpose in every step. I am not just shadowboxing. I discipline my body like an athlete, training it to do what it should" (1 Corin. 9:25–27). Everything we go through in this life is meant to mature us and complete us for a greater work. The brother of Jesus captured some very encouraging words for all of us: "Dear brothers and sisters, when troubles come your way, consider it an opportunity for great joy. For you know that when your faith is tested, your endurance has a chance to grow. So let it grow, for when your endurance is fully developed, you will be perfect and complete, needing nothing" (James 1:2–4). Let it grow!

TNT

One of my favorite scriptures is recorded right after the resurrection of Jesus. "Jesus breathed on them and said, 'Receive the Holy Spirit. If you forgive anyone, he is forgiven'" (John 20:22–23). Too many of us live lives that are lacking power and purpose. Here are some tools that will keep you plugged into the TNT (The New Testament), which will outlive you:

- **Forgiveness** keeps blood clots from forming and your arteries clean. This was the first direction given after being empowered.
- A **grateful heart** will keep you focused on a much higher purpose than what is seen. A heart of praise allows you to rise above and learn from every circumstance.
- **Obedience** to the Word holds us hostage to the direction of God. When we are held hostage to the dysfunctions of the world, we become obedient to them. I would much rather be a prisoner for good than a prisoner for evil.
- **Healthy relationships** are important to stay true to your values. "Don't fool yourselves. Bad friends will destroy you" (1 Corinthians. 15:33).

These are a few things to help keep the TNT in your life.

THE FOG OF LIFE

The fog in life can be very dense at times. You can't see your hand in front of your face. The visibility is zero, and when you turn your bright lights on, the glare bounces back in your face. The anxieties escalate as you are uncertain of finding your way out. The fear of the unknown becomes ever present as you move forward into what lies ahead of you. It is extremely hard to navigate in a fog-filled world. It is normal to feel unstable and a little crazy when your mind tries to make any sense of what is going on. Understanding the different things that bring on the fog will help. Major events like disasters, death, divorce, births, graduations, weddings, building or buying a house, job loss, and many more situations are stressors that can bring on a heavy fog. All of these events are life-changing. You cannot reverse what has happened. Accepting and knowing that you can't go back to the way things were will help diminish the fog. Finding a new normal and way to cope will keep you safe and increase your visibility in the fog of life.

MAKING A DIFFERENCE—PART ONE: REMAIN A STUDENT

One of the best ways to make a difference is to have the attitude of a student. Jesus said, "The student is not above the teacher, but everyone who is fully trained will be like their teacher" (Luke 6:40). Here are a few tools we can apply to making a difference:

- **Keep your antennas up:** Everything that happens in life opens a window of opportunity from which to learn and grow.
- **Ask questions:** If we don't understand something, we need to ask for clarification. Too many times, we assume incorrectly.
- **Study:** This is a critically important part of developing our passion to make a difference. The subject of our hearts is waiting to be unwrapped with knowledge and wisdom if we seek it.
- **Organize:** If we don't organize our time, we will never get off the hamster wheel of daily distractions.

MAKING A DIFFERENCE—PART TWO: SPEND TIME ON YOUR STRENGTHS

As we continue unwrapping "tools" to make a difference, today's focus is on developing our strengths and not our weaknesses. We must remain passionate and willing to become the end result. Too many of us spend the majority of our time on our weaknesses instead of our strengths. If we spend our time on our strengths, we become stronger. Conversely, if we spend our time on our weaknesses, we become weaker. So the focus needs to be on developing our strengths. Try the following scale and watch the positive results take place in your everyday life.

How to Spend Your Time Wisely

- **85 percent on your strengths:** Challenge yourself to identify five of your strengths. Once they are targeted, focus on them and develop them.
- **10 percent on something new:** Always challenge yourself to grow and learn something new about yourself and your passions. These things will keep you moving forward.
- **5 percent on your weaknesses:** Weaknesses are important to recognize. Use them to keep you focused on your strengths.

MAKING A DIFFERENCE—PART THREE: STOP BEING AFRAID

Today's focus is on overcoming our fears so we can *remain passionate and willing to become the end result*. Fear is "False Expectations Appearing Real." Fear is all about perception. Instead of thinking about what could go wrong, think about what could go right. Faith is "Fear Ain't In This House." The winner between fear and faith is the one we feed.

- Understand there is a war going on. Feed your faith.
- Change the pictures in your head to positive ones.
- Be thankful for the things in your life from which you can grow and mature.
- Exercising will allow you to escape the mental captivity that accompanies fear.
- Talking helps. "As iron sharpens iron, so one person sharpens another" (Prov. 27:17).

MAKING A DIFFERENCE—PART FOUR: DO SOMETHING

Take decisive and immediate action. It doesn't matter if you are a genius, highly educated, uneducated, or displaced, you can't change anything or make any sort of real-life progress without taking action. Knowledge and wisdom are both useless without action. There's a huge difference between knowing and doing.

- **Connect with a passion of your heart:** Your passion will help drive you to make a difference.
- **Break it down:** Breaking passion projects into steps makes everything doable.
- **Create a timeline:** Timely goals will help keep you motivated.
- **Support:** Surround yourself with people who believe in you and can help you fulfill your passion.
- **Record your progress:** Collecting data will help you see where you came from and where you are going.
- **Reflect:** Make sure you are on track with your intended purpose.

BE A CAN OPENER

Grocery stores are filled with canned goods. We walk up and down the aisles to pick out things to fill our cupboards. The cans have an expiration date and need to be opened before that date so the contents will still be good. Many people are living lives that resemble canned goods on a shelf. The world is full of unopened goods that have an expiration date. We are all created to be good and do good. One of the best things we can do in life is to be can openers and help open the lids on other people's goods. The best way to do that is through an act of kindness. The intentional act of removing people's lids not only opens their potential but allows us to be part of something much bigger than we could imagine. By opening others, we open the opportunity for God. "In the same way, let your light shine before others, that they may see your good deeds and glorify your Father in heaven" (Matt. 5:16). Look for opportunities to be a can opener before the expiration date we are all faced with.

LOVE, THE GREATEST GIFT

Have you ever loved so much that you felt your heart turn inside out? Have you ever cried so much that your tears stole your every breath? Have you ever been in so much pain that you became immobilized in a fetal positon and you felt you needed a crowbar to separate your limbs? One of the hardest things in life is to have a broken spirit, which causes you to lose the momentum to live, let alone love. Mother Teresa captured something in a quote that took me a long time to understand: "I have found the paradox, that if you love until it hurts, there can be no more hurt, only more love." As I have baked in this thought, I have come to realize that our love can be refined in our darkest minute, hour, day, month, or year. Love is the only thing that can build fiber and tissue around dry, broken bones. Love is the only thing that allows the flow of blood into a lifeless body. Love is the only thing that can bring back a desire to live again. Our Lord learned to love through the pain of hurt. The true hurt was being separated from His dad: "My God, My God, why has thou forsaken me?" (Matt. 27:46). In our separation from those we love, we can learn the paradox of "only more love." My dad died in my arms, and it was the darkest hour of my life. But I now know that the greatest gift my dad gave me was his last breath. Love through the pain!

LOVE TRANSFORMATION—PART ONE

My pastor touched on something that was word transformational. It involved changing a noun into a verb. Two of my favorite scriptures are captured in two sentences, with a total of six words: "God is love" (1 John 4:8) and "Love one another" (John 13:34). The first sentence uses *love* as a noun, while the second sentence uses *love* as a verb. My kids grew up watching the *Transformers,* which showed a noun (automobile) turn into a something capable of acting on its own (verbs). Once we understand that *love* is a person (noun), we can let it transform us into an action. When love becomes an action, it transforms us and everything around us. Our world comes alive, and we can have an impact in it. *LOVE* can be an acronym for "Living Outside Vulnerable Experience." I love this acronym because *living* is an action, *outside* is something beyond myself, *vulnerable* is being exposed, and *experience* is an understanding. *Love,* the verb, means being able to live beyond my circumstances as I become vulnerable and susceptible to experience God, the noun. God transforms us through His love.

LOVE TRANSFORMATION—PART TWO

Pastor Daniel Winn used an analogy of an old steam train in relation to marriage. The engine in the front of the train is moved by the energy of steam from the burning of coal. The cars behind are used to haul things—what they are depends on the purpose of the journey. The train has a caboose at the end. In significant relationships, we are moved by the combustion of throwing love into the furnace and allowing the relationship to be fueled by it. The power of love is lessened when we focus on the cars that we are hauling over time. The cars could be kids, debt, separate interests, work, different goals, hobbies, and so on. Before we know it, we are in the caboose with very little hope for survival as the cars are now controlling our destination. There is only one way to gain control of a runaway train. We must crawl, run, and climb our way to the front engine and throw our love into it. The cars of life all represent vulnerable experiences. Living Outside a Vulnerable Experience allows love to regain control of our direction and destiny. Get out of the caboose and let love control you. My favorite sentence in the Bible is, "God is Love" (1 John 4:8).

THE GREATEST COMPLIMENT

One cold winter's day, a ten-year-old boy was standing barefoot in front of a shoe store, peering through the window, and shivering with cold. A lady approached the boy and asked him what he was doing. "I was asking God to give me a pair of shoes," the boy replied. The lady took him by the hand, went into the store, and asked the clerk to get a half dozen pairs of socks for the boy. The clerk returned with the socks. After placing a pair upon the boy's feet, she then purchased him a pair of shoes. She tied up the remaining pairs of socks and gave them to him. She patted him on the head and said, "No doubt, my little fellow, you feel more comfortable now?" As she turned to go, the astonished lad caught her by the hand and, looking up in her face with tears in his eyes, answered the question with these words: "Are you God's wife?" It is amazing how one act of kindness can be an answered prayer. We never know the power of God and how He can use us in the smallest way. Be on the lookout for God's purpose. Ask for one divine appointment a day.

GREAT
TIME TO REMODEL

My wife loves to rearrange the furniture all throughout the house. I always resist the change, but once I get used to it, the house feels fresh and alive. The scriptures give us several examples of a house that is changed. When Jesus went to Zacchaeus's house, "Jesus said to him, 'Today salvation has come to this house, because this man, too, is a son of Abraham. For the Son of Man came to seek and to save the lost'" (Luke 19:9–10). When Jesus went to the centurions, he said, "Truly I tell you, I have not found anyone in Israel with such great faith" (Matt. 8:10). Then, when Jesus went to Lazarus's house, "Jesus called in a loud voice, 'Lazarus, come out!' The dead man came out.... 'Take off the grave clothes'" (John 1:43–44). When we invite God into our houses, we might be initially resistant, but once we get used to it, the house is fresh and alive with faith, hope, purpose, salvation, and—my favorite—new life. As for me and my house, we will serve the Lord.

BURNT FRIENDSHIPS

One of the toughest hurdles in life is to get back on your feet after miscommunication occurs between friends. "An offended friend is harder to win back than a fortified city. Arguments separate friends like a gate locked with bars" (Prov. 18:19). When we are hurt by words, actions, or events, the pain can be so severe that we see, feel, and respond as a result of the pain we are in. Reactions and responses that are rooted in hurt almost always have negative results and consequences. Relationships that go south can have the same devastating effects as death. Many of us have to learn to keep moving forward with unresolved conflict. Forgiveness is powerful for soul healing, even if the other person is unresponsive. Every burnt relationship we have experienced can make us stronger if we let it. Forgive yourself, forgive others, and keep moving forward in humility.

WHAT'S IN MY BUCKET?

The book *How Full Is Your Bucket?* provides a great picture of the interactions in relationships. Every one of us has a bucket and ladle. We are at our best when the bucket is full and overflowing, and we are at our worst when the bucket is empty. Our ladles can either pour into someone else's bucket to fill it or dip into and empty it. Whenever we fill someone else's bucket, we in turn fill our own. If we choose to talk negatively about people, we drain them and ourselves. If we choose to say something positive, we fill their bucket and ours. Whatever is in my bucket is what I give. If my bucket is full of anger and fear, my relationships are going to be splashed with anger and fear. If my bucket is full of love, my relationships will be soaked with love. So the question we need to ask ourselves is, What's in my bucket? God is love, so ask God to fill your bucket with His living water, and scoop out to others whenever you get the chance.

HOLDING UP EACH OTHER'S ARMS

The battles we face in life are not meant to be fought alone. The enemy uses fear to immobilize us, depression to hold us in bondage to self-defeat and self-worthlessness, and exhaustion to weaken us. Exodus 17 reveals to us an intense battle and the willingness to accept the assistance and resources from others. The Israelites were encountering their first opposition while wandering in the desert. The Amalekites, a group of nomadic raiders, attacked the people of Israel. As long as Moses kept his arms up, Joshua had the edge in battle. Eventually, Moses became weary, and so Aaron and Hur responded by placing a stone underneath him to sit on while holding up his arms until the Israelites were able to finally defeat the Amalekites. Each individual mentioned had the help of others. Learn to always use the resources and help from others to win your battles.

OBLIGATION TO OPPORTUNITY

Have you ever done something that you didn't want to do and became frustrated for doing it? Then you wake up the next day, week, month, or year and realize you are still doing the same thing. That is an unhealthy obligation. An obligation is something to which a person is bound or obliged to do. An obligation arises out of a sense of duty. Obligations are important until they become unhealthy. If we can learn to change our perception of unhealthy obligations and look at them as opportunities, doors will be unlocked and windows will be opened. As a child, I was forced to attend church and school as they both became daily and weekly obligations. I was rarely mentally present during the obligations and found myself locking onto exit strategies. The perception I had of church and school was negative; I felt confined, like I was in jail. Once I changed my perception of those obligations and saw them as opportunities, my world opened up. What I had once perceived as negative was turned into a positive, and I began to use these obligations to fuel my opportunities. I am humbled to say that I received a doctorate. I can't stop learning and was ordained in 1983, and I am as hungry as ever for the things of God. I challenge you to turn your obligations into opportunities by changing your perception.

NONVERBAL COMMUNICATION: TWO IMPORTANT PIECES

Appearance: People make their first impression on someone new they meet in the first seven seconds. It is incredibly important that you dress the part you want to communicate. It takes people a very long time to overcome a first impression, if they can at all. Here are seven things to consider in your first impression:

- Adjust your attitude.
- Straighten your posture.
- Smile.
- Make eye contact.
- Raise your eyebrows.
- Shake hands.
- Lean in slightly.

Handshake: A good handshake is also a very important piece of nonverbal communication.

- Too strong of a grip communicates dominance and someone who wants to be in total control.
- Too weak of a grip communicates low self-esteem and poor confidence.
- Straight away is good and appropriate.

- If the hand is on top facing down, it is a sign of control.
- If a hand is facing upward, it is a sign of empathy, understanding, and submissiveness.
- When the web of the palm touches the other person's web of the palm, it means the person is comfortable with him- or herself.

SOMETIMES OUR PLANS DON'T WORK OUT

When we look back at past situations, we realize that God had something better in mind for us or that we weren't ready to handle what we were asking for. More than forty verses in the Bible reference waiting on the Lord. After thirty-three years of pastoring, I wanted to retire and move to be with my older kids and grandkids. My wife and I strategically set up a plan to "get out of Dodge." Four major things had to happen, and we thought all four would be slam dunks. Well, I retired, and we waited out a very frustrating year, after which we ended up zero for four. How could this be? We had worked and planned so hard to be with family. The plan was perfect, but my mother had a stroke and we needed to stay put. I transitioned into an incredible job where I am fully utilizing my skill set to help others. Our kids, who were still living with us, had some medical procedures that were handled by extremely competent physicians. In retrospect, we realized the reason for our poor record, according to our plan. Remember this: 1) continue to set out your plans, 2) keep a good attitude, and 3) be grateful every step of the way. If things don't come to fruition the way you want them to, be patient and accept the opportunity to learn and grow.

THE FIVE CS

Conflict resolution is a buzz phrase regarding learning how to get along through the speed bumps of relationships. Recent studies have shown that the majority of relational conflicts are a result of misunderstandings (about 85 percent), and the others (15 percent) are disagreements. If the majority of our conflicts are misunderstandings, then we can do something about correcting them. We can work toward a win/win solution if we apply the five Cs.

- **Clarify perceptions:** Open yourself up to the other person's view of the situation.
- **Compromise:** Begin to work toward the middle to create a win/win solution.
- **Choose:** Decide on the most favorable option together.
- **Challenge:** Each person involved needs to accept the challenge.
- **Commitment:** The follow-through is the integrity it takes to make it work.

LIFE'S BIGGEST COMPETITOR

Outrunning and outdistancing an opponent doesn't mean you ran your best race. In order to be your best, you must compete with yourself. Life's real contest is in the stadium of our own mind. A winner is a loser if he or she loses the battle within him- or herself. A loser is a winner if he or she conquers the battle within him- or herself. Our true victory isn't on the field; it is in the head. Victory over others may be the very thing that contributes to the winner's demise. Here are some things to help you win the battle:

- **Lose the arrogance:** Always look to others as better than yourself.
- **Lose the independence:** It's not about you; it's about the team and the cause.
- **Lose the critical spirit:** We must build each other up, not tear each other down.
- **Use every experience** in life to mature and complete you.

RELATIONSHIPS ARE GOOD

If we can look at our relationships throughout life and be grateful for them, we are well on our way to leading a life of gratitude through every event and circumstance. Staying positive and looking for opportunities to live rather than obligations to survive sets us up for wonderful encounters with others. Paul, the apostle, wrote a letter while in one of the most difficult storms of his life. He started the letter with,

> I thank my God every time I remember you. In all my prayers for all of you, I always pray with joy because of your partnership in the gospel from the first day until now, being confident of this, that he who began a good work in you will carry it on to completion until the day of Christ Jesus. It is right for me to feel this way about all of you, since I have you in my heart. (Phil. 1:3–7)

These words are incredible as they talk about a partnership. This partnership brought Paul joy and confidence as he knew that the end result would be a completion of a work that began together. He ended the statement with an assured feeling in his heart. What a way to live—being thankful for our relationships. Relationships are good!

RUN FROM TEMPTATIONS

I remember growing up hearing "Danger! Danger!" while watching *Lost in Space*. We must be aware of our danger zones and avoid knowingly putting ourselves in bad "space." A wise sailor knows when the storm is more than his or her boat can handle. Here are some tools to help you sail through the waters of life:

- Keep your eyes on the horizon to see any storm clouds that are forming.
- Steer clear of bad waters that feed into the storm.
- Turn your rudder and sail in a different direction.
- Keep your eyes on the peaceful waters and don't look back.
- Use your compass, coastline, lighthouses, and sirens to stay on course.

GOD'S LOVE IS LIKE BLEACH

A woman in Illinois began ministering to children from divorced families, attempting to heal their wounds and pain. One of the illustrations that she did for them was this: She put water in a mason jar, filling it about halfway, and explained that the water represented the substance of their lives. The counselor then had the children squirt little vials of food coloring into the water in accordance with their pain, anger, and hurts. Some would squirt in only a couple of drops; others would almost violently put in as much as they could. In the end, the water would be black from the spread of the food coloring. It was black because no light could get through. Scriptures refer to God as being the Light of the World. He can't penetrate a heart that is clouded with hatred, anger, and pain until forgiveness is poured into the heart. The counselor then poured bleach into each darkened mason jar. The bleach cleared the darkened water much like God's love clears our darkened hearts. God's love for us helps us pour out forgiveness for others so that our hearts can be once again pure and clear before His eyes and the eyes of others around us. God's love is like bleach that cleans our hearts and lets light shine through our darkness.

GLOW

A person who "GLOWs" is one who will bring light into a dark world. The world is starving and searching for those who can make a positive difference in the lives of others. The following acronym will offer a guide to live your life illuminating everything in your path.

- **Give:** "A generous person will prosper; whoever refreshes others will be refreshed" (Prov. 11:25). Giving is an attitude of the heart. If we can ingrain giving into our heads, hearts, and hands, it will become a habit that will enliven others. When we refresh others, we will be refreshed in return.
- **Love:** "Let love and faithfulness never leave you; bind them around your neck, write them on the tablet of your heart. Then you will win favor and a good name in the sight of God and man" (Prov. 3:3–4). Love is contagious as it illuminates your heart.
- **Observe:** "The things you have learned and received and heard and seen in me, practice these things, and the God of peace will be with you" (Phil. 4:9). Peace will follow those who learn and observe and apply.
- **Wait:** "They who wait for the LORD shall renew their strength; they shall mount up with wings like eagles; they shall run and not be weary; they shall walk and not faint" (Isa. 40:31). Learning to wait patiently for things will increase your glow.

RESPECT

Respect is a cornerstone of relational growth in the personal and professional world. Here is an acronym we can use to apply to our everyday lives,

- **R**esponsibility: One of the foundations of respect is being responsible for our actions both professionally and personally.
- **E**mpowering: This is the ability to make others around us feel confident, strong, capable, and competent in their jobs.
- **S**upport: This is when we anticipate needs and expectations and build on a *wow* experience for our fellow associates.
- **P**ositive: This is when we work hard and tackle challenges in a positive and encouraging way.
- **E**nthusiasm: A huge part of respect is a zeal and passion for ourselves and others in the interest of the workplace and at home.
- **C**ommunication: Respect is critical in the communication process as it allows us to listen and understand when messages are so often misunderstood.
- **T**eam: Team building is positively associated with high morale, high productivity, and high profitability. Team respect is also associated with physical and physiological well-being.

CHOOSE
YOUR RESIDENCE

I want to paint a picture of three residences with a bridge between them. Imagine two circles—one above and one below—with lots of room on the outside of them. There is a cross between the two circles. The vertical part of the cross has a portion inside the bottom circle and a portion in the upper circle. The horizontal part of the cross is exposed to everything outside of the two circles. Everything outside the two circles represents the world we live in. The bottom circle represents the laws of the Old Testament. The top circle represents the light of the New Testament through grace, mercy, and truth. The cross represents the life, death, and resurrection of Jesus. The arms of the cross, extending to the world, are a bridge to enter into the light of the New Testament. The length of the cross is a bridge to enter from the laws of the Old Testament into the light of the New Testament. All paths from the cross lead *one way* into the New Testament. Thank you, Jesus, for the gateway to God. When we travel the path of the cross into the New Testament, we become the light of the world. It's time to choose your residence.

ENCOURAGE SOMEONE TODAY

Have you ever had a smile, a kind word, or a kind act make your day? The comfort and support of someone else can lift us out of the deepest hole and get us back on the road. I am a beneficiary of recent medical research. There is a bone-bonding compound that looks like toothpaste. Once it is injected into the body, it hardens and reaches the compression strength of natural bone. It is so close to the real bone that the body doesn't reject it. The compound has proved to allow patients to resume activities more quickly and with less pain toward healing and recovery as prior to the surgery. As a result, my back is stronger. An encouraging word or action has the ability to strengthen broken hearts and spirits with a compound that will help the recipient walk and move forward more quickly with less pain. Encourage someone today. Our kind words or acts today may help someone, without our needing to see the result. Thank you for being a gift for someone.

IT'S OKAY TO SAY NO

I was invited to a middle school that was previewing a new course in sexuality along with other parents. I was amazed that the course paid *very* little attention to abstinence or refraining from sexual activity. I voiced a concern and was met with laughter and disbelief. One of the parents even suggested I get my head out of the sand. I sat quietly pondering the situation. The group took a break for cookies and refreshments, and the attendees were asked to put on name tags and introduce themselves to one another. I sat alone during the break waiting for the group to come back around the table. The teacher then said, "We are going to give you the same lesson we are going to give your kids." Everyone was asked to peel off their name tags and look to see who had the dot on the back of his or her name tag. One of the parents raised her hand. The teacher then commented that the dot represented a sexually transmitted disease. Everyone who had shaken hands and greeted one another had then became infected. The teacher said, "Since we all shook hands, we all have the disease." I had to interject that the lesson was awesome and a great way to teach the kids about STDs. But not everyone was infected. I didn't have a name tag or shake hands as I chose to sit back during the break.

STOP THE DAM FROM BURSTING

Picture a little boy trying to stop several small leaks in a dam with his fingers and toes to prevent it from bursting. Solomon wrote, "The start of a quarrel is like a leak in a dam, so stop it before it bursts" (Prov. 17:14). A person who starts a quarrel here and there will someday be the source of an eruption of major proportions. A trickle that becomes a torrent starts out as more water flowing than predicted, which leads to water flow that is impossible to control. The burst then leads to water that will never be retrieved. So the solution is to not allow the dam to be breached. James wrote, "I'll be swift to hear, slow to speak, pushing down my anger for the Lord" (James 1:9). To prevent a flood, the best thing to do is shut up!

HHH—PART ONE:
HEAD, HEART, HANDS

As we all try to embrace transitions, I want to share with you the most important source of life we have, the Word of God. F. B. Meyer, one of the history's great Bible teachers, writes, "Read the bible not as a newspaper, but as a love letter. If a cluster of heavenly fruit hangs within your reach, gather it. If a promise lies upon the page as a blank check, cash it. If a prayer is recorded, launch it as a feathered arrow from the bow of your desire." Why the Bible? In a world where trust is in short supply, the scriptures tell us, "Not one word has failed of all the good promises he gave" (1 Kings 8:56). In thirty-three years of preparing sermons every Sunday, the most important lesson I have learned has been to keep my head, heart, and hands all on the same page, glued to the Word of God. The very best thing I can offer to you and myself is to reinforce the importance of these God-given body parts' working together. "Love the Lord your God with all your heart and with all your mind and with all your strength" (Mark 12:30). Let's explore these words of Jesus.

HHH —PART TWO: HEAD, HEART, HANDS

Our thoughts consume us. The average adult makes thirty-five thousand choices a day, all of them anchored in the mind. Our thinking is influenced by a myriad of things—emotional, physical, and spiritual. Some of the things that come at us throughout the day are uncontrollable, but other influences are controllable. Controllable or not, it is very important to have our thoughts anchored. That is why Jesus said, "Love the Lord your God with all your heart and with all your *mind* and with all your strength" (Mark 12:30, emphasis added). Scriptures teach us to break down every thought and proud thing that puts itself up against the wisdom of God. "We take hold of every thought and make it obey Christ" (1 Corin. 10:5). Learning to control our thoughts begins with loving God with *all* of them. A number of years ago, a bracelet that had "WWJD" engraved in it became very popular. What a great way to examine our thoughts—"What would Jesus do?" If we can hold our thoughts captive to the scriptures and examine them to see if they would mirror our Lord's, we can be well on our way to making godly choices throughout our day.

HHH —PART THREE: HEAD, HEART, HANDS

Jesus talked about uniting three parts of our bodies: head, heart, and hands. "Love the Lord your God with all your heart and with all your mind and with all your strength" (Mark 12:30). For us to have complete balance and enjoy a good night rest, our hearts, heads, and hands all need to be on the same page. The heart is the source of our emotions. One of the best ways to keep our emotions healthy and focused is to love God with *all* of them. This is an intentional act that requires a disciplined focus. When the events and circumstances of life stir our emotions, the best choice is to love God with them immediately. If we can anchor our hearts in the Lord, we will not only survive the waves of emotions but be guided by His presence. "For where your treasure is, there your heart will be also" (Matt. 6:21). Our hearts not only sustain us physically but lead us emotionally. Find ways to connect your heart to the heart of God. "May these words of my mouth and this meditation of my heart be pleasing in your sight, Lord, my Rock and my Redeemer" (Ps. 19:14).

HHH —PART FOUR: HEAD, HEART, HANDS

The actions and behaviors of our hands are connected to our hearts and heads. Everything we do is dictated by a thought or an emotion. Our hands execute our desires, wishes, and needs. That's why Jesus said, "Love the Lord your God with all your heart and with all your mind and with all your *strength*" (emphasis added). Our hands and actions represent our strength. "Whatever you do, work at it with all your heart, as working for the Lord, not for human masters, since you know that you will receive an inheritance from the Lord as a reward. It is the Lord Christ you are serving" (Col. 3:23–24). Sometimes, the only thing people will see and judge us on is our actions. We may have only one chance to represent the Lord. Loving God with *all* our heart, head, and hands will bring integrity and character into our lives. When what I think, what I say, what I feel, and what I do are all aligned in the Lord, we will have and lead lives of purpose and worth. Practice, practice, practice, over and over, the uniting of your HHH. You will sleep better, and your tank will be full.

THE ROLLER COASTER OF LOSS

I've heard it said that when you lose a parent, you lose your history; when you lose a spouse or sibling, you lose your present; and when you lose a child, you lose your future. The pain of losing someone you love or care deeply about is extremely difficult to navigate. I often think of the grieving process as a roller coaster. The grind of the uphill climb takes you up and over into an uncontrollable descent. Then come the whiplashing curves that toss you from side to side only to lead to the grinding climb again. Each day is filled with the emotions of climbing and falling and all the twists and turns of surviving one day at a time. The only things that keep us from falling all the way out are a seat belt and safety bar. The seat belt and safety bar must be fastened and secured for us to survive. The fiber of the seat belt and the composition of the bar that hold us are made up of the things that we can't see. The things we see will fade away, but the things we can't see will last forever. That's why we never give up. Allow faith to begin to fill the empty cave of your being. Hold on to its handlebar and fasten its belt around your waist as you begin the uphill grind of facing the roller coaster one second, one minute, one hour, and one day at a time.

GPS: GUIDE THROUGH PERSONAL STORMS—PART ONE: THREE STORMS OF LIFE

In our journey through life, we are always in one of three seasons on the road we travel. We are driving *into* a storm, driving *in* a storm, or driving *out* of a storm. The duration of the storm, whether we are going into, inside of, or out of a storm is dependent on the event or circumstance. The season could last for minutes, hours, days, weeks, or years. The two common threads to understanding all three seasons are that we are always surrounded by storms and we are driving. Picture yourself as an automobile. There are all kinds of elements outside your vehicle that will affect your drive. There are also all kinds of circumstances and events on the inside of your vehicle that will affect your drive. "GPS" helps us identify the things we can control and the things we can't control. Understanding the things we can control can help us stay between the lines and out of the ditch. Being aware of the things we can't control will help guide us through the stressors of life that bring anxieties, worry, tension, pressure, strain, trauma, and hassle. I have spent a lifetime of offering roadside assistance along with tending to my own flat tires and personal ditch experiences. Whether offering assistance or needing assistance, the GPS coordinates of guiding your thoughts, guiding your day, and guiding your life will help you navigate.

GPS: GUIDE THROUGH PERSONAL STORMS—PART TWO: GUIDE TO CONTROLLING OUR THOUGHTS

The biggest fight in our lives involves what is in our heads. The things we think about can consume us and hold us hostage, or they can set us free. The mind is the most powerful tool in our lives. The most difficult task we will ever face is learning how to control our thoughts rather than allowing our thoughts to control us.

An old Native American legend talks of a chief who was very powerful and led his tribe and life with conviction and passion. The chief's grandson sat on his lap one day and said, "When I grow up, I want to be a brave warrior and chief just like you." The grandpa looked down at his grandson and said, "Son, there are two wolves in this life. There is a bad wolf, and there is a good wolf. The bad wolf will growl at you, chase you, and pin you down. He will put you in a corner and not let you move. He will manipulate you and fill you with fear and guilt so that you will be paralyzed, immobile, and in prison. Then there is a good wolf. He will walk beside you and protect you. He will guard you at night when you sleep. He will always be on the lookout for anything or anyone that is out to get you. He will be your companion and your strength." So the grandson looked up at his grandpa and asked, "Which wolf wins?" The grandfather and brave chief said, "Whichever one you feed."

What thoughts are you feeding?

GPS: GUIDE THROUGH PERSONAL STORMS—PART THREE: GUIDE TO NAVIGATING THE DAY

Lou Holtz is a former Notre Dame football coach. Always a great motivator, Holtz once gave an inspiring talk while addressing his players about his three rules of life. His speech has motivated me in navigating my daily life. Three of his rules that now guide my day are as follows:

1) When you wake up, give it all you've got.
2) Do the right thing.
3) Help someone.

Let's talk about applying these three rules to our lives.

1) **Give it all you've got:** Growing up as an athlete and student, I was taught to give it 110 percent or more. The reality of this statement makes no sense. We can only give what we have. If you have only 30 percent, give it 30 percent. The key here is to give whatever you have.

2) **Do the right thing:** Studies have shown that the average person makes thirty-five thousand choices in a day. Each choice tends to piggyback on the previous one. Think about it. When we open our eyes, the choices begin. *Am I getting up on the right side of the bed or the wrong side of the bed?* The power of our choices can make or break a moment, minute, day, year, or sometimes our entire lives.

3) **Help someone:** If we can train ourselves to constantly have our antennas up and be tuned in to ways we can help people, our days will be fulfilled. Have you ever had someone say or do something for you that served as a breath of fresh air in a polluted environment? A word, a phrase, or an act of kindness can help someone come out of a ditch.

GPS: GUIDE THROUGH PERSONAL STORMS—PART FOUR: GUIDE TO BEING MOTIVATED

Now we turn our focus to a guide to move us and motivate us through our day. As we navigate our personal vehicles through the storms of life, I want you to think of the tires as having three spokes. The spokes make up three equal parts of the circle of the tire. The spokes are physical, spiritual, and emotional. When one of the spokes is missing or neglected, the tire is compromised and the performance is affected. The result is a bumpy ride, which can cause very serious alignment issues. We need to balance our tires (physically, emotionally, and spiritually) to make sure we have a smooth ride. As a first responder, I witnessed countless disasters that included mass fatalities. I have seen thousands and thousands of personal vehicles (our personal life vehicles) blown, swept, and pushed into the ditches of life. As a counselor, I have seen thousands of individuals who have experienced personal disasters that have sent them into the ditch. We need assistance in realigning our tires at times, and many resources are available to assist us. Here are just a few:

- **Emotionally:** Counselors, books, cards, words of encouragement
- **Physically:** First responders, doctors, physical therapists, rehab
- **Spiritually:** Scriptures, churches, spiritual leaders

If your days are bumpy and you are having difficulty being motivated, check your alignment.

GPS: GUIDE THROUGH PERSONAL STORMS— PART FIVE: MILE MARKERS

In ancient times, mile markers or milestones were used to mark the distance along certain paths of travel. They came in all different shapes and sizes and were usually separated by a specified distance and identified by numbers. In the United States, we have adopted a mile-marker system that can be seen on the sides of our highways. The mile markers have numbers on them and can assist us in our travels. The mile markers help identify where we are, where we are going, and from where we have come. They also provide critical information to first responders in determining the locations of accidents along with coordinates for those in need of roadside assistance. We all have our personal stories that warrant the use of mile markers. In regard to our personal "Guide through Personal Storms," mile markers will be useful tools in guiding us while we drive into, drive in, and drive out of the storms that surround us. Establishing our personal markers will take a concentrated effort in identifying important events, circumstances, and roadside assistance we have received, are receiving, or will receive. Whether traveling daily, weekly, or yearly, these markers will help us in navigating old roads and new roads. Everything that has happened to us has gotten us to where we are so that we can prepare for where we are going. These markers will remind us of our past so we can be present for our future.

EYES OF FAITH

Having faith means more than just believing. It is being able to see beyond the things that are seen. When we have faith in God, we know without a doubt that God will keep His word and His promises. We persevere in our faith through hardships, pain, and persecution. In our faith, we know where we've come from, where we are today, and where we will be tomorrow. Faith is anchored in our past, present, and future. It gives us the ability to focus on the things beyond that are a result of things present and past. There is comfort in every season of life when we have eyes of faith.

- External
- Yearning
- Eternal
- Sight

Our eyes of faith give us an External Yearning for an Eternal Sight.

IRREGULAR PEOPLE

There are going to be people who rub us the wrong way. Many of these people are in our inner circle, and we can't get away from them. Let's define them as impossible but unavoidable relationships. Every one of us has at least one irregular person or persons in our lives— manipulating mothers, frictional fathers, corrosive companions, abrasive aquaintances, merciless mates, grating grandparents, sandpaper siblings, hard-hearted husbands, or worthless wives. How important are these relationships to us? Do we walk away from them? Do we manage them from a distance? Do we face them and work them out? The thing that most often breaks down in an irregular relationship is communication. Communicating is the only method we have for changing the situation or the person. We have to choose our battles wisely. I have learned to manage the irregular people in my life in different ways. Talking out our differences and trying to resolve the friction is necessary with my family and inner circle. In the case of associates and friends, I have learned to accept them the way they are and not be controlled by them. The worst disease in human nature is not being understood or wanted. Good luck!

FOUR "TUDES"

Attitude with gratitude leads to latitude with altitude. In other words, a thankful heart gives you the freedom to fly above any circumstance. Following is a paraphrased part of Robinson Crusoe's journal entry after being shipwrecked on an island for twenty-seven years. Let's call his lists the baditude list and the gratitude list and compare the two.

- **Baditude:** "I'm stuck on this island without any hope." **Gratitude:** "I wasn't drowned like the rest of my shipmates."
- **Baditude:** "I've got no clothes." **Gratitude:** "It's too hot to wear clothes anyway."
- **Baditude:** "I've no way to protect myself from man or beast." **Gratitude:** "I'm glad I am shipwrecked here and not Africa where the wild beasts are."
- **Baditude:** "I've got nobody to talk to." **Gratitude:** "God sent the ship in near enough to the shore that I've gotten out so many necessary things that will enable me to supply myself as long as I live."

Wow! Our reality is made up of the things we focus on. That's *wisdom*!

March 21

TICKLE ME

(From my three-year-old daughter's perspective)
Well, I'm just a baby and I like to play.
I could stay outside and goof around all day.
When the friends come over, they all say hello.
They pick me up and tickle me and won't let go.
They tickle me and tickle me and squeeze me tight.
If you don't let go, I'm going to give you a bite.
I'll pull your hair and bite your nose and fingers too.
Or I'll hold my breath until I turn blue.
I like to play ball with my dear old dad.
I hit him in the head and he gets mad.
But he doesn't stay mad for very long
'cause he picks me up and sings me this song.
I like to watch Mommy while she does her chores.
I like to push the vacuum all over the floors.
When the work's all done for the rest of the day,
she picks me up and tickles me and says, "Come on! Let's play!"
The day's all done and I'm so glad.
No more tickles from Mom or Dad
They put me to bed, but I can't sleep.
I even try to count those wooly sheep.
Tomorrow can't possibly be a bore
'cause they'll pick me up and tickle me and love me some more.

KIDS TAKE TIME

A coach and mentor to my kids said something once that stopped me in my tracks: "Treat all kids fairly, but never treat them equally." As I pondered this, I realized its validity and truth. We are all created unique and different, and whether we are parents, guardians, teachers, or coaches, we must find ways to motivate, discipline, and educate our kids differently. It is good to set boundaries and mile markers for kids, but getting them to stay between the lines and moving forward requires awareness. The only way to learn how to effectively communicate while guiding and leading our kids is to look into their eyes and hearts and find out what makes them tick differently than others. The ability to reach inside them and speak to them takes time and effort to develop. My twin boys are uniquely different, and it is a journey to learn how to motivate them to reach their goals. Disciplining is different as well. We have learned that giving rewards and removing privileges has a different effect and outcome based on their desires and needs. Whatever role we have in kids' lives, we must take the time to get to know them before we can have an authentic impact. Thank you, Coach Martin, for helping me slow down to learn and listen.

WAIT—
CHANGE IS COMING

Are you waiting to find a solution to a problem? Are you struggling because things aren't falling into place for the change you desire? Have you noticed that when you get what you want, you are still waiting for something else? Have you ever said, "I can't wait for this to be over"? The fact is, we live in a world diseased with *me-itus*, where we eat when we're hungry, we buy anything we think we need, we chase things that aren't good for us, and we make quick decisions that ripple into other decisions, which eventually snowball into a rock at the bottom of a hill. This fast-paced "give me what I want" society is ambushing the things God has in store for us. We are being bred and conditioned with a drive-through mentality to not wait for anything. Consider the long process of a butterfly evolving from its cocoon. If we try to rush God's purpose and process, we can produce something that is deformed and can't get off the ground to fly. Job said, "All the days of my life I will wait till my change comes" (Job 14:14). We've heard it said that good things come to those who wait. The real question is, Who are you waiting for? What God has for you is worth more than any season of waiting or any price you have to pay. He won't disappoint you. Wait—change is coming.

THREE INGREDIENTS TO WALK TOGETHER

When in a covenant relationship, there are three ingredients that must exist for the parties to walk together: beliefs, values, and lifestyle. If we can get all of these components on the same plate at the same time, there can be a side-by-side union.

- **Beliefs:** Belief is the ability to connect the mind with the heart. My dad taught me early on that the hardest eighteen inches to bridge in life are between the mind and the heart. Once the two are connected, there is a foundation for trust, confidence, and faith in something or someone.
- **Values:** Values in a relationship include ethics, morals, standards, principles, philosophies, and guidelines. Values are the anchor to our being and soul. They are the core of our existence. They are the foundation of our integrity, which connects our thinking, feeling, and doing.
- **Lifestyle:** Our lifestyles are defined by the way we live. They include our habits, customs, traditions, practices, recreational activities, hobbies, attitudes, tastes, and spending tendencies. Lifestyles define and separate people. In a relationship, a lifestyle defines, forms, and predicts a living environment.

The combination and balance of these three ingredients will allow two people to walk together.

ELIMINATING PREJUDICE

While channel surfing during a sleepless night, I stumbled on a talk show featuring representatives of the Ku Klux Klan. The most disturbing part of this bottom-feeding talk show was a six-year-old boy wearing one of the cone hats. Prejudicial words of hate and anger spewed from this child's mouth. I was emotionally moved to witness the influence of his dad and others who were on that stage. Prejudice is symbolized by a plethora of terse descriptions, bad opinions, attitudes, values, thoughts, and actions. Prejudice often manifests in hostile and resentful emotions toward certain people. We are all influenced by the attitudes of a decaying world that is full of hate and discord fueled by prejudice. The only way to eliminate and overcome prejudice is to renew our minds. We must flush the unreasonable thoughts of judgment down the toilet and into the sewer where they belong. Be kind to one another. A world without prejudice may be impossible, but we can choose to *not* partake. We must look past the outward differences and see the beauty of what lies within. Eliminating prejudice begins with one person. Paul's advice is perfect: "Get rid of all bitterness, rage and anger, brawling and slander, along with every form of malice. Be kind and compassionate to one another, forgiving each other, just as in Christ God forgave you" (Eph. 4:31–32).

A SPARK OF DANGER

A spark on dry timber can unexpectedly cause a firestorm that can burn thousands of acres of land. Words of gossip have the same ability to destroy friendships, relationships, and reputations. These word firestorms can come out of nowhere and consume the very lives of people we love and care about. The spread of rumors is seldom helpful or uplifting. Gossip usually centers on negative information about the private affairs of others. We can learn to control our tongues by not saying anything negative or bad about anyone.

> When we put bits into the mouths of horses to make them obey us, we can turn the whole animal. Or take ships as an example. Although they are so large and are driven by strong winds, they are steered by a very small rudder wherever the pilot wants to go. Likewise, the tongue is a small part of the body, but it makes great boasts. Consider what a great forest is set on fire by a small spark. The tongue also is a fire, a world of evil among the parts of the body. It corrupts the whole body, sets the whole course of one's life on fire, and is itself set on fire by hell. (James 3:3–6)

The consequences of fiery words are too hurtful to others. Don't be a spark of danger.

RAINBOWS BRING HOPE

Rainbows are beautiful things to witness through the drops and mist of a storm. There are some very interesting dynamics of a rainbow. The sun is always behind you when you face a rainbow, the rain is in the direction of the rainbow, and the circular arc of the rainbow is in the direction opposite of the sun. The sun is a symbol of warmth and life as we become dependent on it for survival. As the sun shines behind us in our storms of life, a rainbow is illuminated and becomes a source of beauty and comfort. It allows us to focus on something beyond the circumstances behind us. The rain and storms of our lives flow and pour in the direction of the rainbow, giving us an understanding that the things we are going through will turn into something we can't imagine. The circular arc allows us to see the path directly opposite of the storm as it becomes a covering of and entrance for a new direction. The sun illuminates, the rain guides, and the arc provides direction. When our gaze is on the rainbow, we can easily forget the storm we have come through. The rainbow provides hope and direction from the journey behind us.

THREE RULES OF LIFE

I have had the honor of being a husband, dad, coach, instructor, pastor, counselor, and friend. Lou Holtz, former Notre Dame football coach, has motivated me and thousands of students and athletes with three rules of life. In summary; 1) give everything you have to the best of your ability, 2) do the right thing, and 3) show people you care. Every person can apply these three principles while navigating the daily race that each of us runs. When applied, these rules will give the average person the ability to succeed and be fulfilled at the highest level.

1) Put everything you have on the field and play through the whistle. Whether at work, home, or play, give it your all emotionally, physically, and spiritually.
2) The average person makes thirty-five thousand choices a day, and many of them depend on the previous one. If we can purposefully do the right thing, good things will follow.
3) People around us will respond positively and favorably if they know they are cared for. When we go out of our way to benefit someone else, the rewards are intrinsic.

These three rules will allow us to push through our days from the inside out. The speed bumps that we face during the day may slow us down, but we will keep moving.

INTENTIONALLY NEGATIVE PROGRAMMING

On that sleepless night when I was channel surfing and came across the show about the KKK, I found myself feeling so sorry for the six-year-old boy who was spewing hatred out of his mouth. He had been contaminated by his father. King Herod also experienced negative programming.

> On his birthday, Herod gave a banquet for his high officials and military commanders and the leading men of Galilee. When the daughter of Herodias came in and danced, she pleased Herod and his dinner guests. The king said to the girl, "Ask me for anything you want, and I'll give it to you." And he promised her with an oath, "Whatever you ask I will give you, up to half my kingdom." She went out and said to her mother, "What shall I ask for?" "The head of John the Baptist," she answered. At once the girl hurried in to the king with the request: "I want you to give me right now the head of John the Baptist on a platter." (Mark 6:21–25)

An intentionally negative influence is one of the most difficult challenges to overcome. Once it is detected, new core values can erase the pollution.

THUNDERSTORM OVERSPRAY

Have you ever driven on an interstate during a thunderstorm with pounding rain? The vehicles around you, including semis and cars, add more drama with the spray of their vehicles onto your windshield. In fact, the windshield wipers cannot go fast enough when traveling behind a large vehicle that is causing a lot of spray. The important thing to understand is that the other vehicles are not intentionally making the storm worse. As we go through storms in our personal lives, a lot of people around us will add drama or trauma to the situation unintentionally. People can say things and do things that can hurt us, just like the overspray on the interstate. Be careful to not hold people accountable for something they have done to you during a storm. Keep the windshield wipers on until you get through it. Too often, we hold people responsible for things they did not mean to do. Keep in mind that the overspray from your own vehicle has the same effect on others around you as well. Let's get through the thunderstorm together without adding extra tension to the drive.

DON'T GIVE UP YOUR DREAM—REVISE YOUR PLAN

Have you ever had the wind blown out of your sails in regard to your career or your calling? Sometimes we need to step back and approach things differently. General George S. Patton Jr. said, "Successful generals make plans to fit the circumstances but do not try to create circumstances to fit plans." If we become too focused and locked onto a clear plan to reach our potential and destination, we can close the door to other opportunities. Our inflexibility can cause us to stick to "the plan" no matter what and derail us from the end result. Sometimes it is best and wiser to explore other options on the way to the finish line. Don't give up on your dream; revise your plan. As author and management consultant Peter Drucker said, "The question that faces the strategic decision maker is not what his organization should do tomorrow. It is, 'What do we have to do today to be ready for an uncertain tomorrow?'" We can do certain things that can help us face the challenges and uncertainties of tomorrow:

- **Put your faith in God:** King David wrote, "The steps of a good man are ordered by the Lord." There is an anchored divine peace when we let God be in charge.
- **Learn to be flexible:** Flexibility opens up windows that appear to be closed.
- **Learn to adapt:** "The only way to make sense out of change is to plunge into it, move with it, and join the dance" (Alan W. Watts).

EAT TO LIVE
VERSUS LIVE TO EAT

A few years ago, I was diagnosed with type 2 diabetes. I was on insulin and eventually moved to pills instead of the injections. The most difficult thing about controlling diabetes is the diet. I had lived my entire life loving food and never having to worry about carbs or any dietary issues. I had developed a perception of food that I lived to eat. Food began to dictate major decisions of my day. If I wasn't thinking about food, I was planning where I could go. I grew up in Las Vegas, the mecca of buffets. I lived for the buffets and would often go alone if no one could join me. My perception has since changed, and I have to keep reminding myself of it. I know now that I must eat to live. I have lived on a roller coaster of shifting back and forth based on my A1C results. If I have good numbers, I cheat and fall back into living to eat. When the numbers increase, I shift back to eating to live. This is a constant battle that I face. The lifestyle change from living to eat to eating to live must take place for survival. Join me in accepting a healthier outlook as I commit to eating to live.

THRIVING IN BATTLE

There is a constant war for your defeat on three major fronts: the world, your body, and your spirit. It is a battle of good (God) versus evil (Satan). The world has a desire to swallow you in its quest for power, self-promotion, and popularity. Scriptures teach us to avoid becoming swept up into the world's obsession. We are to be the influencers, not the influenced. The battle for the body has a loud voice as it yells in your face that you don't look good, you don't feel good, and you are going nowhere. We fall prey to self-destructive addictions and diseases that beat our bodies down. Scriptures teach us that we're hard pressed on every side but not crushed, perplexed but not in despair, persecuted but not forsaken, and struck down but not destroyed—and that's why we never give up. Satan's attack on our spirits is constant. Understanding his ways equips us to handle his attacks. Scriptures teach us to put on the "armor of God" so we can stand our ground.

Stand firm then, with the belt of truth buckled around your waist, with the breastplate of righteousness in place, and with your feet fitted with the readiness that comes from the gospel of peace. In addition to all this, take up the shield of faith, with which you can extinguish all the flaming arrows of the evil one. Take the helmet of salvation and the sword of the Spirit, which is the word of God. (Eph. 6:14–17)

God's Spirit, who is in you, is greater than the devil, who is in the world. Jesus won the victory over evil. Now be encouraged to thrive in battle.

ROADBLOCKS IN RELATIONSHIPS

How do you rate yourself in building relationships? Are people naturally drawn to you, or is there debris on the road preventing access from both directions? Here are a few things that could prevent people from entering onto a common road with you:

- **Moodiness:** Moods are like roller coasters that have highs, lows, and wild turns. If people never know what to expect from you, they will stop expecting anything.
- **Perfectionism:** Unreal expectations are concrete barriers. People respect the desire for excellence but may resist when their chins can't meet the height of the bar.
- **Pessimism:** People don't like to have their sunny days rained on by someone who sees storm clouds.
- **Arrogance:** Nobody wants to be in a relationship with someone who thinks he or she is better than everyone else.
- **Insecurity:** If you are uncomfortable with yourself and who you are, others will be too.

A NEW ALPHABET TO LEARN

I am going to suggest a few words to soak and absorb that are in alphabetical order. Words are very powerful tools to learn, appreciate, and communicate with. These are just a few words that have power to transform a new year:

- Acceptance, achievement, allow
- Balance, blossom, breath
- Caring, compassion, confident, challenge
- Dream, determination, dynamic
- Embrace, empower, energy, enthusiasm
- Forgiveness, fun, faith, fresh
- Gentle, grateful, grace
- Happy, humble, humor
- Improve, inspire, invigorate
- Joy, jump
- Kindness, kiss
- Laugh, listen, love
- Meditation, motivation, music
- Nurture, nature, nourish
- Open, optimistic, overflow
- Passion, positive, purpose, patient, peaceful
- Quiet
- Radiant, reflective, refresh
- Simple, strength, survive, smile, sincere

- Thankful, thoughtful, trusting, tolerant
- Understanding, unselfish, uplifting, useful
- Visionary, valued, vibrant
- Warmth, wellness, worthy
- Yoga, youthful
- Zest, zeal

Now I know my ABCs. Next time won't you sing with me?

INTEGRITY AND CHARACTER HAVE THE SAME FOOTPRINT—PART ONE

Integrity and character walk beside each other when what I think, what I say, what I feel, and what I do are all on the same page. There is a terrible price to pay for lack of integrity. So fearful were the ancient Chinese of their enemies to the north that they built the Great Wall of China, one of the seven wonders of the ancient world. It was so high that they knew no one could climb over it. It was so thick that nothing could break it down. Then they settled back to enjoy their security. But during the first one hundred years of the wall's existence, China was invaded three times even though the enemy never broke down the wall nor climbed over its top. Each time, they bribed a gatekeeper and marched right through the gates. According to the historians, the Chinese were so busy relying upon the walls of stone that they forgot to teach integrity to their children. We must learn at a very young age that integrity and character have the same footprint.

INTEGRITY AND CHARACTER HAVE THE SAME FOOTPRINT—PART TWO

Scientists now believe that a series of slits, not a giant gash, sank the *Titanic*. The opulent, nine-hundred-foot cruise ship sank in 1912 on its first voyage, from England to New York. Fifteen hundred people died in the worst maritime disaster at the time. The most widely held theory was that the ship hit an iceberg, which opened a huge gash in the side of the liner. But an international team of divers and scientists recently used sound waves to probe the wreckage, which is buried in mud under two-and-a-half miles of water. Their discovery proved to be very interesting. The damage was surprisingly small. Instead of the huge gash, they found six relatively narrow slits across the six watertight holds. Small damage, invisible to most, can sink not only a great ship but a great reputation. When we allow our integrity and character to have small slits, we are doomed to sink. We must allow our integrity and character to walk in step with each other.

THREE GIFTS FROM HEAVEN—PART ONE: CLAY POT, SWORD, GLASSES

I want to unwrap three gifts from heaven: a clay pot, a sword, and a pair of glasses. These gifts are individual and unique in their use and understanding. The first gift is the clay pot. Scriptures talk about our being formed by the potter's hand. "We are the clay; you are the potter; we are all the work of your hand" (Isa. 64:8). It was customary to conceal treasure in clay jars, which had little value or beauty and did not attract attention to themselves. So if God has formed us into His clay pots, we must have a way to shine. In the words of Jesus, "Let your light shine before others, that they may see your good deeds and glorify your Father in heaven" (Matt. 5:16). Jesus also pointed out that a clay jar may be full of light, but the light is concealed unless there is an opening to allow others to see it. When the pot is cracked through imperfections, the light comes out. God's light shines through us in our imperfections so that others can see His work.

THREE GIFTS FROM HEAVEN —PART TWO: CLAY POT, SWORD, GLASSES

In scripture, the sword is referred to as a spiritual weapon representing the truth: "Take the helmet of salvation and the sword of the Spirit, which is the word of God" (Eph. 6:17). When we hold the sword by its handle, it becomes an incredible tool of power and direction as it creates a path before us, much like a machete cutting through a jungle. Our miscommunications, misunderstandings, misdirections, and missed opportunities are like a sword. The blade has the power to do as much damage as it does good. The sword will either cut us or serve us depending on whether we grab it by the blade or the handle. Throughout life, we must learn the difference between the handle and the blade. Hold the handle and allow God to lead you in His Word.

THREE GIFTS FROM HEAVEN —PART THREE: CLAY POT, SWORD, GLASSES

Glasses are a valuable resource to correct vision. Our prescriptions allow us to focus on things near and far. If we see things through the eyes of God, we can have his perception as we focus on His things near and far. "The eyes of the LORD are on the righteous, and his ears are attentive to their cry" (Ps. 34:15). There are some good things that come from looking through God's lenses.

- Rather than feeling the pain people are causing, feel the pain they are in.
- Rather than seeing the fires people are setting, see the fires they are in.
- Rather than expecting a gift, be the gift.

These three gifts can teach us and guide us when applied in God's way. Let the light of Christ fill your clay jar so He can shine through your imperfections, hold the sword of truth by its handle and not the blade, and put on God's glasses so you can see things the way He wants you to.

IN HOPE, WE BELIEVE TOGETHER

There are times when our eyes are so teared, foggy, and blind that we can't see or focus on anything except the pain, hurt, anger, or frustration we are in. Sometimes we rely on others' *hope* to help guide us. Hope Opens People's Eyes to see beyond the events or circumstances that surround us and consume us. There have been times in my life when I couldn't see and, honestly, didn't want to see. During these times, I have had family, friends, and sometimes people I don't even know scrape mud off my windshield and give me something to live for. Hope empowered me to see and focus on something beyond the pain. When my dad died in my arms, I lost a huge part of my existence. It took my wife and others to help me see beyond. Since my dad lost his earthly body suit, I have been with hundreds of people, comforting them as they took their last breaths. There is power in *hope,* and we can be part of the empowering process if we believe together. I have committed to carrying windshield wiper blades at all times.

IN FAITH, WE WALK TOGETHER

There are times when we get the wind knocked out of us, and we need one another. Sometimes we have to be there holding each other's hands, wrapping our arms around someone's shoulders, using a wheelbarrow to push, using a rope to pull, and sometimes doing and saying nothing. There are times when we exist because somebody is beside us. Unexpected, tragic loss of life is one of those times. I have seen middle school and high school students huddled in a circle, crying and leaning on one another after a fellow student completed suicide. I have witnessed high school students rally beside one another at the tragic, accidental loss of a fellow student. I have experienced young men come together after the horrific news of losing a former high school buddy. I have encountered families who must walk beside each other in family loss. I have facilitated support groups of parents living with loss, survivors of violent crimes, and people who have lost pets. I am connected to a core group of professionals who have devoted their lives to helping people walk through their deepest, darkest times. The bottom line is that we need one another. In FAITH (Fear Ain't In This House), we walk together.

IN LOVE, WE EXIST TOGETHER

There isn't a person alive who hasn't either experienced having or known someone who has an empty tank. When we are empty, it is hard to think, feel, and act. Countless things drain us physically, spiritually, and emotionally. LOVE, or Living Outside a Vulnerable Experience, is the source of fuel for our existence. When others love us outside a vulnerable experience, it fills our tanks. This could be a parent who continues to love me when something I have done or not done has caused pain and hurt. The unconditional love from our moms and dads can fill our tanks. It could be a friend or associate who still accepts me in spite of poor choices or behaviors. It could be learning to love and forgiving myself despite living in a dark tunnel. The dark place could be a result of something I did or something I inherited. The darkness could be a result of guilt from an accident or a self-destructive decision that someone we care for committed. Love is the only thing that can fill us in our times of emptiness. My favorite scripture is three words: "God is love" (1 John 4:8). In *love*, we exist together.

A PERMANENT MARKER

One of my favorite tools in life is a small dry-erase board, about the size of a small picture you could hang on a wall. I have grown particularly fond of its use in teaching and coaching. In teaching, an overhead projector allows me to convey information by simply wiping the dry-erase board between the messages. In coaching from the sideline, the dry-erase board allows me to demonstrate plays one after another. What happens when a permanent marker is accidentally used? The eraser no longer works, and the message becomes distorted. In life, we start out with a clean dry-erase board. Different events, circumstances, and experiences happen beyond our control and leave permanent marks. These marks begin to accumulate over time, and the messages we send and receive become distorted and unreadable. These are our lives, and we can't erase the permanent marks left on our boards. If we can step back and allow God to connect the marks, He will be able to send His message through us. Every permanent mark has a purpose in the overall messages we send and receive. Accept these permanent marks and allow them to complete the person you are to be. God can turn a mess into a message.

FAITH VERSUS
IMMEDIATE GRATIFICATION

A man parched by the hot sun on a desert journey came across a water pump with a jug that had enough water for a few swallows. The note attached to the jug said that if he primed the pump with the water, he would have all the water he needed and then some. The man had to make a decision between satisfying his immediate thirst with a few sips or believing the words and using every drop of water in the jug to prime the pump and get more. What would you do? We live in a world with a fast-food mentality that has generated decision making based on immediate gratification at the drive-up window. The man decided to trust and primed the pump. Water came flowing in abundance to satisfy his thirst and the ground he was standing on. He put a few sips of water back in the jug and added a P.S. to the note: "Believe! It really works!"

EASTER: SAME EVENT, TWO RESPONSES— PART ONE: THE GOOD VOICE

One of the world's most significant events is recorded in the twenty-eighth chapter of the book of Matthew. It was very early in the morning as the sun rose. "There was a violent earthquake, for an angel of the Lord came down from heaven and, going to the tomb, rolled back the stone and sat on it" (Matt. 28:2). This event was witnessed by two different groups of people, believers and nonbelievers. The first group was represented by a few women who believed in the power of God. They were extremely afraid but were comforted by the voice of the angel telling them to come in and look to see that Jesus had risen from the dead just as He said He would. They were comforted in their fear and told to go and tell the others what they had seen. On their way, they met Jesus, fell at His feet, and began to worship Him. Jesus reassured them of His peace and presence. He then told them to continue their journey. The event they witnessed rocked their world. They were comforted and counseled by a good voice of peace and understanding.

EASTER: SAME EVENT, TWO RESPONSES— PART TWO: THE BAD VOICE

The second group that witnessed this traumatic event was a group of soldiers. They weren't just ordinary soldiers; they were the elite of the centurions who were assigned and paid to watch over the grave of Jesus. Their job was to make sure that nothing happened graveside. They too felt the earthquake and witnessed the angel of the Lord. "The guards were so afraid of him that they shook and became like dead men" (Matt. 28:4). Fear gripped the soldiers just as it gripped the women. In their fear, they ran back to the chief priests who had commissioned them to guard the tomb and told them everything they had witnessed. The elite soldiers were then bribed with a large sum of money and told, "You are to say, 'His disciples came during the night and stole him away while we were asleep.' If this report gets to the governor, we will satisfy him" (Matt. 28:13). So the soldiers took the money and had to wrestle with this deepest, darkest secret. They were paid off and told to lie and to go in hiding. The event they had witnessed rocked their world. They were directed and counseled by a bad voice of deceit.

EASTER: SAME EVENT, TWO RESPONSES—PART THREE: GOOD VERSUS BAD

I want to spend some time processing the two ways scripture tells us that people responded and reacted to a traumatic event. We too are faced with the same kind of opportunity to react and respond to crisis. We can respond as believers in God, or we can respond as believers in something else. Fear is a common response in times of trouble whether we are believers or not. The question then is, where do we run in our fear? If we model our reactions and responses after that of the women, we too can fall on our knees and worship at His feet. His peace will comfort us and guide us in our trial as He tells us to keep moving in our journey. If we model our reaction and response after that of the soldiers, we will run and take whatever bribe is available to cover up and buy us out of what we have experienced. We will then hide behind the events and circumstances. The pain, fear, and emotions of the incident will be hidden and stored away within us. The things that are hidden will consume our thoughts and eventually control our behaviors. Jesus said, "I am the way and the truth and the life" (John 14:6). Allow the truth to set you free. Follow His voice, and you will find His peace every step you take in your journey.

TRANSFORMED, RENEWED, AND RESURRECTED

One of my favorite scriptures is recorded in 1 John 4:4: "Greater is he that is in you, than he that is in the world." The results in our lives should not be determined by what goes on around us. Our results and outcomes should be established by what goes on within us. Events and circumstances can gain a stronghold on us if we are not secure in our internal core values. Paul wrote, "Do not conform to the pattern of this world, but be transformed by the renewing of your mind. Then you will be able to test and approve what God's will is—his good, pleasing and perfect will" (Rom. 12:2). By getting God into our core and adding the passions and beliefs of our hearts as additional ingredients, we become controlled by His desires and will for us rather than the desires and will of the world. The world we live in has some very unhealthy and unwise patterns that are always competing for our thoughts. God has given us the power over our options and the choices that follow. Use the power with Him to overcome the power without Him. Be transformed, renewed, and resurrected from the deception of this world.

AM I RUNNING, OR AM I ON THE RUN?

Am I chasing, or am I being chased? Am I pursuing, or am I being pursued? Every one of us shares a common adversary that is in active pursuit of us, seeking to keep us from moving forward and living up to the fullest potential that we were created for. Our battles are in our heads, hearts, and hands, not the situations or events that flatten our tires. If I am parked, the rearview mirror is useless. The key to a victorious life is to keep moving forward in the chase for God's heart and plan. Use the rearview mirror as a tool to see where you have come from. "As the deer pants for streams of water, so my soul pants for you, my God. My soul thirsts for God, for the living God" (Ps. 42:1–2). Push the pedal to the metal and keep moving forward.

IT'S OKAY TO BE SICK

Have you ever been so sick that you felt like you were being pulled through a keyhole? The worst part is when you are in the middle, with half of you on one side and the other half on the other side. You know you must get on the other side of the sickness, but you're stuck in the middle with no energy, motivation, or desire to move. Sometimes when that happens, it is best to do nothing but veg in the quietness of nothing. You should know what to do physically, so here are a couple of suggestions on what to do mentally. First, give yourself permission to be sick. You live life at a hectic pace, and most of us don't take time to slow down and rejuvenate our bodies, minds, and souls. You feel guilty if you're not running on the hamster wheel or if you say no to or cancel obligations. Taking a break to heal is critical, and you deserve this downtime. Second, don't blame yourself. You didn't do anything wrong to cause yourself to get sick, and guilt will only make you feel worse. Sometimes you just get sick. It's not because you didn't exercise, meditate, eat right, or take the right supplements. Sometimes you're just sick. This is your time to be ill. Accept that it is temporary and you will soon be back to your regularly scheduled program.

SOAK

One of the best ways to make a difference is to have the attitude of a student. Jesus said, "The student is not above the teacher, but everyone who is fully trained will be like their teacher" (Luke 6:40). Here are a few tools we can apply to make a difference when we SOAK in learning:

- **Study:** This is a critically important part of developing our passion to make a difference. The subjects of our hearts are waiting to be unwrapped with knowledge and wisdom if we seek them.
- **Organize:** If we don't organize our time, we will never get off the hamster wheel of daily distractions.
- **Ask questions:** If we don't understand something, we need to ask for clarification. Too many times, we assume incorrectly.
- **Keep your antennas up:** Everything that happens in life opens a window of opportunity from which we can learn and grow.

FAITH AND TRUST LEAD TO EACH OTHER

Have you ever noticed that when you have faith in something, you put your trust in that something? We believe a chair will hold us, so we put our trust in it when we sit down. We believe our cars will start, so we trust the ignition when we turn the key. We believe in the power of light, so we put our trust in the light switch as we flip it on. Faith is a springboard for trust. Faith allows us to jump, and trust allows us to fly. Faith comes alive only when we trust in what we believe. Faith is dead without works, and works are dead without faith. If you are struggling in your relationships, it is usually because there is an absence of one or the other or both. I know that my leap of faith into the arms of Christ has allowed me to trust in Him and His Word. If I am building above a sinkhole, I must relocate to "higher ground."

TOUCHED

I was the celebrant for a recent funeral and graveside service. The spirit in the chapel was one of celebration as the deceased was honored for her accomplishments during her ninety years. She was quite the sewer and knitter. Prior to the start of the celebration of life, I asked the daughter of the deceased if the scarf she was wearing was handmade. It was beautiful! When I reached the part of the service where I highlighted the skills of her hands, I walked over to the daughter and asked if I could wear the scarf. I placed it around my neck and finished the service, after which I returned it. We all went to the graveside and paid our final earthly respects. At the conclusion, the daughter put the scarf around my neck and told me she wanted me to have it. She then gave a handmade quilt to our funeral director. In her grieving, she wanted us to have a keepsake of her mom's. In thirty-seven years of doing funerals, this was a first for me. We got *wow*ed by *wow*ing the family we served. Priceless! These are the touching moments that fill our tanks in continuing to help others in their darkest hours.

AM I A RINGLEADER OR A RUNGLEADER?

Let's examine these two different leaders and see what kind of a leader you are. A ring is a circle that holds someone within its boundaries. A rung is one of the horizontal crosspieces that form the steps on a ladder. The crosspieces in life are made of events, circumstances, and situations that happen to us or others we know. As they form, they can be wrapped in perceived injustice or perceived value. These crosspieces consist of loss, pain, hurt, turmoil, stress, anger, joy, love, peace, and a wide array of emotions and experiences. Ringleaders use the crosspieces of life to lead people with selfish ambitions and motives. Rungleaders, however, use the crosspieces of life as footholds to lead people in stepping up to unknown heights. If the crosspiece is used as a weapon of offense or defense, we build our lives inside the circle with an agenda that holds ourselves and others hostage. My ringleading influence is all about me. If I use the crosspiece as a tool to learn, mature, and complete myself, it will become a rung on the ladder of life. The greatest leader of all time used rungs for Himself, climbing to heaven's door and unlocking it through His resurrection. His example allows us to do the same. In the words of His brother, "Consider it pure joy whenever you face trials of many kinds" (James 1:2). The rungs help develop our faith, which leads to perseverance, which leads to maturity, which leads to our God-given potential. Are you a ringleader or a rungleader?

PASSION, PERSEVERANCE, PURPOSE

Have you ever finished something because you knew you had someone in the shadows rooting you on? Have you ever gotten strength from a crowd of people who have been there and done that? Have you ever been all alone and all you had is what was in your gut? Have you ever felt deserted with nothing in the tank to keep you going? All of us will at some time be strengthened by the faith that others have in us. All of us at some time must face the lonely journey of having to gut it out. There is an eternal motivator that will keep your engine running on the coldest of nights. There is an eternal motivator that will move mountains. Jesus relied on it to get to the finish line, and so must you and I. "Because of the joy awaiting Him he endured the cross" (Heb. 12:2). If we can fix our eyes on Jesus, He will pioneer and perfect our faith. The catch to this is, "The joy of the Lord is my strength" (Neh. 8:10). His joy fuels my passion, perseverance, and purpose.

SOCIAL MEDIA'S EFFECT ON RELATIONSHIPS

In relationships of the past, people had little to no communication with others unless it was face to face. Connections were made in person, first impressions were permanent, and opinions were pure. It was very difficult to hide behind a screen. Conversations took place in person, and feelings were openly observed. Commitments were easily made because there were no outside distractions or influences on personal relationships. With the emergence of technology and the invention of social media, relationships have been drastically affected. What was once awkward, difficult, or uncomfortable to say in person is now easy to type and hit send. At one point in time, people could live their relationships without constant pressures, expectations, and onlookers. Social media has magnified these stressors and has caused anxieties and a sense of distrust. What once was private and personal has now become public to unwanted onlookers. Couples feel a need to validate and build up their relationships on social media in order to fit in with the expectations society has set. Social media's original intent of healthy communication has turned into a cesspool of unhealthy emotional responses, such as jealousy, insincerity, anger, and distrust. What once was meant for good has been polluted. By becoming aware of the effects of social media, we can detour the negative paths and stay on track for healthy relationships.

PREPARING FOR BATTLE

The war is on. It is a battle for the minds, hearts, and hands of people—between the forces of good and evil, between God and Satan. The male species of the Alaskan bull moose battle for dominance during the fall breeding season, literally going head to head with antlers crunching together as they collide. Often the antlers, their only weapon, are broken. The heftiest moose, with the largest and strongest antlers, triumphs. Therefore, the battle fought in the fall is really won during the summer, when the moose eat continually. The one that consumes the best diet for growing antlers and gaining weight will be the heavyweight in the fight. Those that eat inadequately have weaker antlers and less bulk. Likewise, spiritual battles await us as Satan roams and seeks to destroy. Will we be victorious, or will we fall? So much depends on what we do now. The bull moose principle applies: enduring faith, strength, and wisdom for trials are best developed before they're needed. We don't fight for the victory; we fight from the victory that Jesus gave us. The next few weeks, I will be covering the spiritual armor that is necessary to walk in victory.

QUIET TIME

(Author unknown)
I needed the quiet so he drew me aside
Into the shadows where we both could hide
Away from the bustle, where all the day long
We hustled and worried and hurried along
I needed the quiet but at first I rebelled
But gently, so gently, my cross He upheld.
He whispered so sweetly of spiritual things
Though weakened in body my spirit took wings
To heights never dreamed of when active and gay
He loved me greatly, He drew me away.
I needed the quiet, no prison my bed
But a beautiful valley of blessing instead
A place to grow richer, in Jesus to hide
I needed the quiet so He drew me aside

PROVIDER

Whether parents or children, teachers or students, employers or employees, we are created with a purpose to benefit others in reaching their full potential. John Maxwell embraces our role as *providers*.

- **P**urpose: We approach others with a purpose to help them develop.
- **R**elational: We are created to love God and people with our heads, hearts, and hands.
- **O**bjective: We assess strengths and weaknesses objectively and always try to do the right thing.
- **V**ulnerable: We remain open, honest, and transparent.
- **I**ntegrity: We are examples of what we teach.
- **D**ependable: We are consistent, responsible, and available.
- **E**mpower: We give power away and facilitate growth in others.
- **R**esourceful: We use every tool we have to grow people.

"Do nothing from selfish ambition or conceit, but in humility count others more significant than yourselves. Let each of you look not only to his own interests, but also to the interests of others" (Phil. 2:3–4).

SMALL, STILL VOICE

I was recently in downtown Chicago using my GPS, when the voice started spitting out different directions at every intersection. I spent an hour circling tall buildings and congested storefronts only to find myself right back where I had started. I called the destination in a frustrated panic, and the operator gently said, "Turn off your GPS. They don't work downtown. Now look to your right. We are the tall building you're staring at." I realized that the resource I had become so dependent on had let me down. In the center of giant obstacles, communication becomes scattered. When communication breaks down, fear and panic sneak up on us; we need to *stop* and listen.

> "Go out and stand before me on the mountain," the Lord told him. And as Elijah stood there the Lord passed by, and a mighty windstorm hit the mountain; it was such a terrible blast that the rocks were torn loose, but the Lord was not in the wind. After the wind, there was an earthquake, but the Lord was not in the earthquake. And after the earthquake, there was a fire, but the Lord was not in the fire. And after the fire, there was the sound of a gentle whisper. When Elijah heard it, he wrapped his face in his scarf and went out and stood at the entrance of the cave. (1 Kings 19:11–14)

In the midst of our chaotic and hectic lives, God's voice is there. Turn off the GPS and listen.

PING-PONG

Have you ever been cruising through your day when an intrusive thought came out of nowhere? Sometimes these thoughts are disturbing and conflicting to our core values There is a constant battle going on in our heads. The battle is a constant Ping-Pong match between good and evil. Paul described this battle in his letter to the Romans.

> Although I want to do good, evil is right there with me. For in my inner being I delight in God's law; but I see another law at work in me, waging war against the law of my mind and making me a prisoner of the law of sin at work within me. What a wretched man I am! Who will rescue me from this body that is subject to death? Thanks be to God, who delivers me through Jesus Christ our Lord! (Rom. 7:22–25)

Paul, like all of us, struggled in his thought life. He found an answer to his conflict. The scriptures and our Lord will direct us and guide us to gain control of our thoughts. The evil thoughts will never leave our side, but we can manage them with our relationship with Christ and His Word.

TNT FOR LIFE

When I think of TNT, I think of explosive power. I live very close to a rock quarry where I hear the TNT explode the hardened rocks that are otherwise immobile. It is no different than the hardened hearts of we who are paralyzed and immobile as a result of pain or fear in our lives. The first words Jesus spoke to His disciples while they were frozen in fear were, "'Peace be with you! As the Father has sent me, I am sending you.' And with that he breathed on them and said, 'Receive the Holy Spirit. If you forgive anyone's sins, their sins are forgiven; if you do not forgive them, they are not forgiven'" (John 20:21–23). The first use of the power of the Holy Spirit is to forgive. Forgiveness is the TNT (The New Testament) to loosen hardened hearts. Too many of us are frozen in fear or holding others hostage because of an injustice done to us. The pain or fear keeps us miserable and unable to move forward. Trust in Jesus's words, receive the Holy Spirit, and forgive those who have offended you. Offer mercy as it has been offered to you. Forgiveness is the TNT for life.

EVERY CORE IS SURROUNDED BY SEEDS

Our core beliefs are surrounded by seeds that produce fruit. Those seeds are our thoughts, our emotions, and our actions. Our core beliefs about the world (is it safe or dangerous?), about other people (can we trust them or not?), and about ourselves (am I worthy or unworthy?) are formed early in our lives. Imagine a two-year-old who is hungry, alone, and crying. Also imagine three responses to the child: 1) Parent comforts, cuddles, and feeds the child (I am accepted and loved), 2) parent ignores the child and lets the child cry itself to sleep (I am alone and abandoned), or 3) parent chastises and abuses the child and sends the child to bed (I am unlovable, and people are out to hurt me). How about you? The beautiful option we have in life is to change our core, and the seeds will follow. You are loved!

INTUITION LEADS TO INSIGHT

Most times, our intuition will separate the two competing voices of the good wolf and the bad wolf. There is a constant battle between good and evil, wisdom from above and wisdom from below, and good choices and bad choices. Understanding and leaning on our intuition could save us much disharmony when we put our heads on our pillows. Here are a few examples of responding to the good wolf intuition instead of the bad wolf intuition:

Good Wolf	Bad Wolf
• Safe and secure	• Scary and unsettled
• Gentle and comforting	• Choppy and anxious
• Truth and guidance	• Deception and distortion
• Peace and harmony	• Turbulent and agitated
• Love and kindness	• Contentious and rude
• Reasonable and sound	• Irrational and crazy
• Clean and structured	• Polluted and unorganized

Don't be afraid to listen to your good wolf intuition. It will make a difference in your day, month, year, and life. The fruit of our lives is dependent on the source of good living water. Let your good intuition sustain you.

PROBLEM SOLVING

My twelve-year-old son brought me an anonymous quote: "Instead of telling God how big your problems are, try telling your problems how big your God is!" As my mind swam in that quote, I questioned what motivates me in my problem solving. Am I motivated by need or faith? If I focus on the need, I can easily sink into fear. If I focus on God, I can easily soar into faith. Fear (False Expectations Appearing Real) is a silent anchor to death, while faith (Fear Ain't In This House) is a catapult into life. Rather than having my problems speak to me and overpower me, I will speak to the problems and tell them they have no power over me. We can't escape the internal conflict that problems bring. With the power of the Holy Spirit, we can manage them in God's way. So the choice is ours—is it the power of our problems or the power of God that will rule?

SETBACKS

Setbacks have the power to destroy us, immobilize us, or teach us a lesson about what to do and what not to do. Like sandpaper, setbacks can smooth out our rough edges. They can chisel away at our hardened hearts. They can be a first step in moving toward something bigger and better that we would never be aware of. Setbacks shape us into our fullest potential. Setbacks reach down into the depths of our souls and expose some deep-seated areas that need some light. If we let them, they will bring new sensitivity and awareness in ourselves and for others. If you are experiencing the pain of loss, take many deep breaths, slow down, and ride the heat of the flames. The flames will diminish and the smoke will clear. Once that happens, you will be able to assess the situation and rely on the peace and presence of God to guide you. Don't be in a hurry. The pain you are experiencing will serve you if you wait for its lesson. "But those who wait on the LORD shall renew their strength; they shall mount up with wings like eagles, they shall run and not be weary, they shall walk and not faint" (Isa. 40:31).

PATIENCE IN THE PROCESS

When I moved from the West Coast to the Midwest, I had to make a huge cultural adjustment to the pace of life. The West offers a hectic, fast-paced lifestyle while riding the hamster wheel of life. The highways are congested and filled with stressful road rage. However, the Midwest evolves around Mother Nature and the seasons she brings. Traffic is slowed down by tractors and trains. The lesson to learn in life challenges, decisions, and direction is to be patient in the process. Whether waiting for the timing of planting or harvesting or being engulfed in the pace of technology, the challenge we all face is patience in the process. Our kids are focusing on the end result rather than the journey to get there. When we're hungry, we eat without waiting for the process of a kitchen-cooked meal. When we are competing in sports we want our Ws and participation rewards before we make the commitment. When we are working, we look for compensation before significance. The food from the kitchen, the wins from commitment, and the significance from our labor are all part of being patient in the process. Slow down and allow the process to train you and equip you for the seasons of life.

ACT OF FORGIVENESS

None have escaped being a recipient or the cause of hurt feelings, anger, or deep-seated ill will. Perceived injustice and guilt have the same crippling effects. We become chained and handcuffed to unforgiveness whether we deserve it or we need to grant it. I watched a friend approach a prosecuting attorney, a defense attorney, and a judge, asking them to lift the death penalty of the man who shot and killed her son. The result of her forgiveness transformed this killer; he stood up and asked her for forgiveness for what he had done and the pain he had caused the family. I watched the mother of the convicted murderer hug the victim's mom because they both wanted to put an end to the pain. The *act* of forgiveness has the power to repair, mend, soothe, heal, and restore broken hearts.

- **Action:** The regret that you feel must be communicated sincerely. It must come from your heart.
- **Concern:** Don't make excuses or blame others for what you did. Take responsibility and be accountable to forgive yourself and others.
- **Transformation:** Meaningful forgiveness should include a commitment that you will not repeat the behavior.

"Forget about what's happened; don't keep going over old history. Be alert, be present. I'm about to do something brand-new. It's bursting out! Don't you see it? There it is! I'm making a road through the desert, rivers in the badlands" (Isa. 43:18). It's time to *act!*

EMPOWERED

One of the greatest things we can do for people is to empower them in their strengths. I am currently working in a position that I was created for. Everything in my job lines up with my core values and passions in helping people get to a better place. I believe that everything I have done in my lifetime has set me up for what I am doing today. This is a great way to wake up, get my boots on, and get after it. I stopped the owner of the company and thanked him for giving me wings to fly. He said, "You already had them." His response stopped me in my tracks and refueled my tank. Those four words went deep into my soul. Not only did he validate me; his words put wind under my wings. A few words of acknowledgment, a pat on the back, and a smile of acceptance can go a long way in empowering people in their passions. If we look for opportunities to empower others, we can make a difference in their lives and in the lives of others. When a person is empowered, the ripple effect will soak those around him or her.

FEAR AIN'T IN THIS HOUSE

Do bad things seem to follow you wherever you go? Scriptures tell of a man who lived in the shadow of his fears and anxieties. His name was Lot, and he lived in an environment that was headed for destruction (Sodom and Gomorrah). Through divine assistance, he had an opportunity to leave his past and move on to something much greater, but his fear (False Expectations Appearing Real) continued to control him as he parked in a pothole (the city of Zoar). His fear caused him to settle for less. The result was that he had to move again as his anxieties followed him. Our fears keep us on the run, and our potential is never realized. Lot eventually made it to the mountain, where he was divinely directed, but the costs were great. I encourage you to change your residence from fear to faith (Fear Ain't in This House). Get to the faith mountain and find a cave with God.

A LESSON FROM DAD

At the ripe young age of 19, I was faced with a very difficult decision. This was one of those life-changing decisions that had many different outcomes. My dad grabbed a deck of cards. He pulled out a dozen of them and placed them on the table. He began guiding me into a conversation of the different outcomes of my choices. Each card represented a different result from the choice. He took notes for each card as we began to determine the best choice. One by one, he had me remove the cards that represented a non-favorable consequence. We whittled the dozen down to three cards that had the most significant impact on my life. We spent more than an hour looking at these final three choices until a final decision was made. My dad spent a few hours with me that day that helped me make the right choice. It was a life lesson for me to take the time to look at all the angles of important decisions. I have raised my kids with the importance of research and understanding of bigger choices that could have a life-changing impact. Thanks, Dad, for slowing me down and helping me make the best choice I could with the information I had.

DO THE RIGHT THING

Jesus told a parable of the good Samaritan; incidentally, our country passed a law related to it. This parable portrays a modeled behavior pattern that is expected from all of us who desire to do the right thing. There are four things that we can do that will help people in times of crisis:

- Allow compassion to govern our hearts. Keep your antennas up for opportunities to help.
- Take the time needed out of a busy schedule. Sometimes it takes time to do what is necessary.
- Use our personal resources. Cash or other personal possessions may be needed to help.
- Get out of the way. Let God do His job once you have done yours.

If we can incorporate these four steps in Jesus's model of behavior, we can love our neighbors the way God designed us to. If we want to make a difference and do the right thing, we must learn to use our heads, hearts, and hands the way Jesus does. May we all be transformed into loving God and people more today than yesterday.

YOUR STORY MATTERS

Every one of us has a story. Some are big, and some are small. Our big stories are made up of our cultures, genders, personalities, belongings, skills, beliefs, victories, losses, and desires. All of these reveal the direction of our lives and help make up the big picture of who we are. They are like cinder blocks. The small stories are the mortar and substances that fill in the gaps of the big stories, while the little stories are the connecting points. They are the glue that pulls everything together. These are the everyday happenings that slip by almost unnoticed. It is the little stories that shape us and mold us. A few of the things that make up our small stories are our attitudes, emotions, fears, thoughts, perceptions, and actions. Our core values are the foundation for our stories both big and small. The important thing to hold tight to is that your story matters.

BREATHE

Have you ever slowed down to take a big breath of fresh air, especially in higher altitudes? It is exhilarating as the oxygen rejuvenates your mind, body, and soul. There are oxygen bars all throughout the country that allow you to be refreshed by inhaling a fresh uninterrupted flow of oxygen. Oxygen tanks are in hospitals, homes, and on the sidelines of major sporting events to assist in the need for fresh air. Whether exhaling or inhaling, we need to breathe to sustain life. One of my favorite scripture ever recorded was from the mouth of Jesus. "He breathed on them and said; "Receive the Holy Spirit'" (John 20:22). Stop, think, and feel the power of these words. When I took these words in, I took on the power of God to change me from within. The Holy Spirit is not only refreshing; He is our life support from heaven. The Holy Spirit provides an inward comfort, peace, and presence that only God can provide. If you haven't slowed down enough to take on the breath of Jesus, I encourage you to. There is an exhilarating and refreshing existence of the presence of God. Breathe in and receive what is being offered.

A MAMA'S FAITH

Have you ever had anyone say something that changed your life? It could have been a phrase, a sentence, or even an encouraging word that you needed to help you get over a speed bump. There is an unidentified hero in scripture. She was an unnamed mom who was driven by desperation, love, and a vision for her kid, who was involved and held captive by evil and bad choices. She had tried everything that was offered in her timeline, but nothing worked! She heard, believed, and chased a man named Jesus because she had vision and faith that He could help. The problem was that 1) she was a woman, 2) she was not Jewish, and 3) she came from a hostile country that was at war with Israel. *Wow*! Can you imagine the faith this woman had to have to jump over those hurdles? When she arrived on scene, she was ignored, chastised, and encouraged to go home, but Jesus took her aside and began a life-changing conversation. After their verbal Ping-Pong match, he said, "You have great faith!" Her daughter was healed that very instant. This woman had crossed barriers, persisted in her driven state, and saw something far better than what was being presented to her. Here is what we can learn from this no-name mama's faith: Don't let obstacles stop you. Persevere through the storms of life, and believe.

THANK YOU, MOM

M is for the miracle of the breath you gave to me

O is for the offering of your life that set me free

T is for the tenderness that has kept my heart so warm

H is for the home that stands through each and every storm

E is for excitement of living each day new

R is for remembering that it all started with you

Thank you, Mom! Thank you, Mom!

You mean much more to me than you will ever see

Thank you, Mom! Thank you, Mom!

The shadow you provide is where I want to hide

M is for magnificent and how proud I am of you

O is for outstanding for all you say and do

T is for terrific as you have stood by my side

H is for my hero for all the tears you've cried

E is for embracing and protecting like a glove

R is for respect for the greatest gift of love

THIRTY-TWO
WAYS TO STAY CLEAN

I **Dashed** an **S.O.S.** up to the Lord,
A **Signal** while in the **Scope** of sin.
A **Tide** of **Joy** came rolling in to **Safeguard** me,
A **Shield** of **Promise**, a **Gentle Touch** from Him.
Shout it out real **Bold** for all the world to **Cheer.**
Our **Fantastic** Lord's a **Dynamo.**
He'll **Wisk** away your sins and make your life so **Purex,**
Soft Scrub your soul as white as **Ivory Snow.**
I'm riding on the **Crest** of a new **Dawn,**
A **Cascade** of **Sunlight** from above.
I took **Close Up Aim** to **Finish** off the sinful **Biz**
A **Pledge** of **Comfort,** a **Fresh Start** from the **Dove**.

TOP TEN THINGS MY MOM TAUGHT ME

My mother taught me *religion*: When I spilled grape juice on the carpet, she instructed, "You better pray the stain will come out of the carpet."

My mother taught me *logic*: "Because I said so, that's why."

My mother taught me *foresight*: "Make sure you wear clean underwear in case you're in an accident."

My mother taught me *irony*: "Keep laughing, and I'll give you something to cry about."

My mother taught me about *stamina*: "You'll sit there 'til all that spinach is finished."

My mother taught me about *weather*: "It looks as if a tornado swept through your room."

My mother taught me *the circle of life*: "I brought you into this world, and I can take you out."

My mother taught me about *behavior modification*: "Stop acting like your father!"

My mother taught me about *envy*: "There are millions of less fortunate children in this world who don't have a wonderful mom like you do!"

My mother taught me about *timing*: "You have five seconds to get into bed." (Author unknown)

HHH TO DDD

Your *head*, *heart*, and *hands* are being *designed* and *developed* to *deliver* a purposeful life. Paul's heart was always set on discipling, training, and releasing believers into making a difference for God and others. He lived and breathed the HHH principle. He helped develop leaders through his works (hands), his words (head), and his passion (heart). As a student, husband, parent, teacher, pastor, and counselor, it has and always will be my desire to do the same with every saint I am allowed to be with in loving God and people more today than yesterday. Yesterday is history. Tomorrow is a mystery. Today is being unwrapped as a present for each of us to walk in, DDD. We are uniquely *designed* to be part of a much greater plan orchestrated by the hand of God. Our everyday journey is *developing* and completing us through every circumstance and event so we can *deliver* a message of hope and faith in our Lord. Let's use our HHH to DDD every day to their fullest.

LIFE SOCKS

Socks cover one of the most vulnerable parts of the body. They are designed to provide an inner protection of the sole inside the shoe as the feet move in every direction. Picture a sock covering your heart as it protects the soul inside the body as your life moves. If my sock is wet and dirty, then my soul is wet and dirty. If my sock is clean and pure, then my soul is clean and pure. "Hatred stirs up trouble; love overlooks the wrongs that others do" (Prov. 10:12). Is your heart sock made of pain, hurt, anger, and unforgiveness? If it is, you will have a life of conflict and unrest. Is your heart sock made of love? If it is, you will have a life of peace that surpasses all understanding. "Love is kind and patient, never jealous, boastful, proud, or rude. Love isn't selfish or quick tempered. It doesn't keep a record of wrongs that others do. Love rejoices in the truth, but not in evil. Love is always supportive, loyal, hopeful, and trusting. Love never fails!" (1 Corin. 13:4–8).

ACCEPT OR REJECT

Have you ever had an encounter or experience with God? Have you ever been in a jam and asked for help, gotten the help, and then moved on, forgetting the trouble you were in and where you came from? In the scriptures, we see back-to-back encounters with two men and two different responses in meeting Jesus and receiving a divine healing. The first man we find is an invalid, a crippled man of thirty-eight years who got healed and walked away without acknowledging the source of his healing. He was later confronted by Jesus, who warned him not to continue in his lifestyle (attitude and mind-set), saying, "Something worse may happen to you" (John 5:14). This man chose to bite the hand that fed him and use his divine experience for selfish gain. He threw Jesus under the bus. We see a different response from a man who understood the divine purpose of Jesus. This man's response was of gratitude and faith. His actions are described as one of the best models of behavior on this side of heaven: "The man took Jesus at his word and departed" (John 4:50). Both men received healings, but the results of their actions were completely different. The second man validated God's intervention, and "he and his whole household believed" (John 4:53). We all face the choice of accepting or rejecting divine interventions. What's it going to be—accept or reject the presence of God?

SCRIPTURES HELP US COMMUNICATE

Eighty-five percent of conflict results from miscommunication. The following scriptures can help guide us in our attempt to resolve conflict in our relationships. These are some action words (verbs) to generate healthy communication.

- **Listening:** We must learn to listen. We each have two ears and one mouth, so we should listen twice as much as we speak. "Everyone should be quick to listen, slow to speak and slow to become angry" (James 1:19).
- **Reflecting:** Take time to reflect on what is being said or sent. "Those who disregard discipline despise themselves, but the one who heeds correction gains understanding" (Prov. 15:32).
- **Speaking Truth:** Truth builds trust, which is foundational in communication. "Instead, we will speak the truth in love, growing in every way more and more like Christ, who is the head of his body, the church" (Eph. 4:15).
- **Pushing Down Anger:** Anger clouds vision, direction, and logic. We must push it down. "In your anger do not sin: Do not let the sun go down while you are still angry" (Eph. 4:26).
- **Confessing:** Taking ownership in conflict is a huge factor in resolving it. "Be kind and compassionate to one another, forgiving each other, just as in Christ God forgave you" (Eph. 4:32).

LEARNING TO GET ALONG

There is not a day that goes by that we are not faced with conflict. The Bible tells us that conflict is good for us because it matures us and completes us. Today's tools are intended to help us remove the land mines in the battlefield of bad communication. Then we can use the tools for heaven's gain and our maturity. If I can teach my kids how to turn what looks bad into something that benefits them and God, I have done my job. "And we know that all that happens to us is working for our good if we love God and are fitting into his plans" (Rom. 8:28). Here are some words of wisdom from Solomon to help us get along: get the facts before answering, be open to new ideas, make sure you hear both sides of the story, listen to what's being said, be honest, think before you speak, be kind in your nonverbal communications, and say kind things.

TWO STRONG MOTIVATORS

Have you ever noticed how the same event or circumstance can trigger different reactions?

The two main reactions I want to expose are hope and fear. When our reactions are anchored in fear, there is a pattern that follows. We usually buy into or sell out to a false expectation. The results are that we lie about surrounding things and end up hiding because of it while retreating in a surrender march. So out of fear we buy, lie, and hide. When our reactions are anchored in hope, there is also a pattern that follows. Hope leads to joy, and joy leads to strength. When we have hope, we can rejoice knowing that the outcome is benefiting a much bigger picture. The joy becomes our strength to stand up and walk toward the situation with strength in a victory march. So what motivates you?

FIGHT THE FIGHT

Traumatic events can build our faith and secure our hope if we let them. One of the most difficult things in life is to face death head on. Most of us will have an experience with a loved one who has passed or will pass with a terminal illness. Here are some helpful words from scripture to assist in the battle. "Though I walk in the valley of the shadow of death, I will fear no evil; for you are with me" (Ps. 23:4). Death is only a shadow.

- **Call in the troops:** Combined faith has divine power to destroy strongholds.
- **Prepare yourself:** Our battle is in our hearts, souls, strength, and minds, not our flesh and blood.
- **Know your enemy:** Our enemy is the spiritual forces of evil in this dark world—fear, depression, stress, anger, and guilt.
- **Go into battle:** Fight the good fight of faith.
- **Use the Word:** Stand on the scriptures.
- **Rest:** "Those who walk uprightly enter into peace; they find rest as they lie in death" (Isa. 57:2).

SOMETIMES
WE MISS THE OBVIOUS

Sherlock Holmes and Dr. Watson go on a camping trip, set up their tent, and fall asleep. Some hours later, Holmes wakes his faithful friend. "Watson, look up at the sky and tell me what you see." Watson replies, "I see millions of stars." "What does that tell you?" asks Holmes. Watson ponders for a minute. "Astronomically speaking, it tells me that there are millions of galaxies and potentially billions of planets. Astrologically, it tells me that Saturn is in Leo. Horologically, it appears to be approximately a quarter past three. Theologically, it's evident the Lord is all-powerful and we are small and insignificant. Meteorologically, it seems we will have a beautiful day tomorrow." Then after a pause, Watson says, "Well, Holmes, what does it tell you?" Holmes is silent for a moment and then he speaks. "Watson, you imbecile, can't you see that someone has stolen our tent?" Sometimes we miss the obvious while trying to observe and figure things out. We need to slow down, take a breath, and look for the obvious things around us before we speak or act.

LEARNING TO BE CONTENT

There is a multibillion-dollar industry designed to get us to buy everything under the sun. The average person is plagued with more than three hundred advertisements a day, all designed to persuade us to do something we don't need to do. John D. Rockefeller was once asked, "How much does it take to satisfy a man?" His answer was, "A little more than he has now." Being content frees us to enjoy what we have versus being owned by what we don't have. How can we fight the craving to have more than we need?

- Make a habit of giving things away.
- Beware of things that feed an addiction.
- Ask yourself, "Can I live without it?"
- And most important of all, have an *attitude of gratitude.*

TWO ACTS HAVE CHANGED MY WORLD

I can't tell you how many times somebody's story has stopped me dead in my tracks and caused me to redirect my day, my week, my year, and my life. Our fast-paced, drive-through mentality and approach to life has disconnected us from so many people and so many things. In my personal journey, I have implemented a couple of daily actions to keep me connected with things that are much bigger and more important than the things I am held hostage to. The first thing is that I ask for one divine appointment a day. This is an appointment from heaven's throne that I have no control over and that I have to be flexible enough to see and respond to. The second thing is to have at least one focused, meaningful, and intentional conversation. This is something I do have control over. I have come to realize that these conversations feed the soul and are the first to escape us when time is scarce. By implementing these two daily requests, my life is richer and fuller than I could ever imagine.

SOMETIMES IT'S BETTER TO SAY NOTHING

Two geese were preparing to fly south when a frog asked if he could go along. The geese questioned how he could do it. "Easy," he said. "You guys hold this stick between your beaks, and I'll hang on with my mouth." Off they went as people looked up, admiring their teamwork. The trio was making great progress until somebody from below shouted, "Great idea! Whose was it?" That's when the frog opened his mouth and yelled, "Miiiiiine!" Every time we open our mouths, there are consequences (*The Word for You Today*). Larry King said, "I remind myself every morning: nothing I say this day will teach me anything. So if I'm going to learn, I must do it by listening." Have you ever noticed that those who like to talk are forever speaking and forever hearing very little? On the other side is the person who is able to listen without having to express knowledge or interject an opinion. If we can build this into our character, we are on a journey of maturity and respect. Sometimes we need to keep our mouths shut.

ARE YOU EMPTY?

One of my favorite life lessons in scripture is recorded by Luke in the fifth chapter. He recounts a story about the difficulty of working endlessly, all day and night, with no results. Jesus was in the boat with an exhausted Simon and fellow fisherman. He encouraged them to try casting their nets one more time. "Master, we've worked hard all night, but because you say so I will let the nets down." When they had done so, they caught such a large number of fish that their nets began to break. I, like Peter, have had times when I hit the end of my day with nothing in my tank except exhaustion, fatigue, and depression. Have you been there? Your outlook is bleak, you can't dream anymore, and you're afraid to do anything because nothing has worked. It's disappointment after disappointment. It could be haunting memories, unemployment, addictions, financial failure, or sickness. You wrestle through sleepless nights and empty nets. There is a still, small voice that is speaking in the depths of your struggles. The voice is saying, "Don't give up," and if you can respond, there is a filling coming your way. Can you take what is left in you and say, like Simon, "Because you say so, I will let the nets down." Invite the divine presence of our Lord, and watch how your situation will change.

FAST-FOOD THINKING WILL POISON YOU

We live in a fast-food society and mind-set. When we are hungry, we eat right away. When we want something, we go into debt and buy it right away. If we are unhappy, we build a quick case against those with whom we are in conflict and dismiss them right away. The results fill our lives with potholes of unresolved conflict, which paves the road for an uncommitted life and a fast-food diet. So when we are unhappy with a school, we change schools, start a new one, or quit; if it's a church, we change churches, start a new one, or quit; a sporting team, we change teams, start a new one, or quit; a marriage, we get divorced, start a new one, or quit; or a job, we resign, start a new one, or quit. The list goes on and on as we attempt to survive the fast-food-junkie mentality of an unhealthy life. The antidote is to fight and not give in to the drive-through quick fixes on every corner of life. "The Lord is my shepherd; I shall not want. He makes me lie down in green pastures. He leads me beside still waters. He restores my soul. He leads me in paths of righteousness for his name's sake. Even though I walk through the valley of the shadow of death, I will fear no evil, for you are with me" (Ps. 23:1–4). Don't quit!

AN ATTITUDE OF GRATITUDE

Attitudes are the strings attached to particular behaviors. Charles Swindoll said, "The only thing we can do is play on the one string we have, and that is our attitude.… I am convinced that life is 10 percent what happens to me and 90 percent how I react to it. And so it is with you.… We are in charge of our attitudes." Did you know that you can choose what side of the bed you're going to get up from? Attitudes will make us or break us. Here is some AA (attitude adjustment) fuel.

- **Choose happiness**: Focus on happy, seek to be happy, and mentally go there.
- **Choose optimism**: Everything has two sides.
- **Choose an open mind**: New information is good.
- **Choose your own thoughts**: Don't choose someone else's.

THE HEAT IS ON

The desert heat is very hard on the paint job of a car. Over a period of exposure to the outside elements, the paint oxidizes. Left unprotected to the brutal UV rays of the sun, the paint will fade away. So the result is a dull vehicle traveling on the roads throughout the course of a day. You won't notice the damage immediately as it occurs over a period of time. Our lives are very similar as we are exposed to the elements of this world that are very hard on us. We are like oxidized cars as our lives become dull and unattractive. The damage is done gradually over a period of time, and before we know it, we are parked in a lifeless parking spot. Paint oxidation is not the kiss of death. A dual process can be done to bring back the luster of the original shine, much like the dual process that can bring back the shine that God originally meant for us. A compound applied to the faded life rubs the contamination and dead particles away. Then a polish comes next to restore the body to a shining state. "Let your (paint) light so shine before all men that they might see your good in works and glorify your Father who is in heaven" (Matt. 5:16). The Word of God provides the dual process of applying the compound and the polish.

TURN THE SWITCH

Usually when I wake up in the middle of the night, I am struggling with unresolved relational issues, personal health issues, or conflict that I intercede for. But early one morning, I woke up with an overwhelming sensation of gratitude. As I lay wide awake, I simply held my bride and began thanking God for her and who she is and all she does. The hour went quickly before the early alarm sounded. More than twenty years ago, I wrote something out that I believe and live by. This was and is my marital mission statement: "I love my wife more today than yesterday." This mind-set has allowed me to fight through the adversity of relational dysfunction that we face in our marriage. The hour I spent in total uninterrupted appreciation for my bride has given me an awareness and thankfulness of the gift she is. I share this to encourage you in your relationships. The frustration and disappointment felt in broken-down relationships can be overturned and overrun by an attitude of appreciation for that person. Whether it is a spouse, a kid, a family member, or an associate, you can change the course of any relationship by turning the switch from obligation to opportunity. You fill in the blank: "I love my _____ more today than yesterday." Turn the switch and let this be your relational mission statement.

SELF-DISCIPLINE FROM THE INSIDE OUT

Self- discipline is the fuel to keep us moving in a positive direction. A friend recently said, "Say no for a short time so you can say yes for a lifetime." What a perfect defining statement of letting self-discipline guide our journeys. Self-discipline must become a lifestyle. It is not a one-time event. It is a short-time commitment that leads to a lifetime habit. If we can anchor our choices in our core values, the priority of our decisions will keep us focused on lifetime results rather than on short-term satisfactions. Part of the success of this is to reward yourself at the finish line instead of along the way. We must learn to eat our vegetables before the dessert. We should not get a participation medal for trying. We should get the rewards for victorious wins at the time of jumping the hurdles in a lifelong race. Don't make excuses along the way. An excuse is an escape from responsibility. Stay focused on the results of the work rather than the difficulty of the work. Focus on the benefits of doing what is right. This is self-discipline from the inside out. Stay true to your core and keep moving in confidence toward your desired results.

DO WE OWN WHAT WE POSSESS, OR DOES WHAT WE POSSESS OWN US?

Many things can motivate us to accumulate wealth and possessions—retirement benefits; fear of losing our jobs; trying to keep up with the Joneses; and a variety of insurance items such as health, home, and life. A lot of these motivators are based on insecurities. We accumulate and amass possessions, thinking that the more we have, the safer we will be. I have spent a lifetime helping people transition from an earthly body suit to an eternal one. One of the most difficult things to hear from those transitioning is how their lives were dominated and controlled by some of the things we mentioned. The reality is that we can't take anything we have with us. The key to not being owned by our possessions, and learning to own them, is to have an attitude of gratitude. Being thankful for everything we own and have is critical to our health and well-being. When we live with this attitude, we replace fear with faith. We live with thankfulness and not need. We are driven by passion and not necessity.

ANGER MANAGEMENT—PART ONE

Studies have shown that people experience the emotion of anger eight to ten times a day. Anxieties, depression, fear, and grief drain the body of physical and emotional energy. Anger releases energy into the nervous system and makes a person ready for action. The difficult part of this release is using the burst of energy in a constructive way instead of a destructive way. Often, anger takes the form of rage, fury, resentment, hostility, and other emotional outbursts. When people hold grudges or are annoyed, irritated, disgusted, frustrated, offended, or infuriated, they are most likely going to experience some form of anger. When anger controls us, it becomes unhealthy. When we can control our anger, it can turn into something healthy. If people are controlled by their anger, they will exhibit destructive behaviors, which could include physical, emotional, and verbal abuse and violence. Healthy anger allows a person to use this same energy and confront the evil, right the wrongs, and turn things around from bad to good. Martin Luther King said, "When I am angry, I can write, pray, and preach well, for then my whole temperament is quickened, my understanding is sharpened, and all mundane vexations and temptations are gone."

ANGER MANAGEMENT—PART TWO

In order to confront and control unhealthy anger, one must commit to a plan of counterattack in advance. We must be in a place where we can think clearly and accurately. If we can understand the power of anger, we can harness it into something productive. The following tools are for us to create a game plan to respond with healthy anger.

- **Be aware.** One myth many believe relating to anger is that anger will show itself through appearance and actions. The reality is that a battle may rage behind a very calm demeanor. People must identify what makes them most vulnerable to anger. Everyone is different.
- **Accept responsibility.** It is very easy to shift blame and hold others hostage for our anger. People don't lose it; they choose it. It is ultimately our choice. That is why it is so important to choose healthy anger.
- **Identify the source.** Anger is a result of something that has happened to me or to someone else. People who hurt feel vulnerable, and that can open the door for more hurt. Identifying frustrating personalities or uncomfortable events and circumstances can help us recognize a root to our anger.
- **Choose a healthy response.** This is a critical piece of anger management. We must find creative and constructive ways to control our response. This means being honest, open, and direct in communicating. It's recognizing truth and righting wrongs.

KNOWING YOUR CORE VALUES

Do you ever struggle with knowing what the right thing to do is? When you know what your core values are, your decision making becomes infinitely easier. Our core values give us a definite picture of the kind of people we want to be and the kind of lives we want to live. When we are in conflict with our values, we lose sleep, become stressed out, or become depressed. People's values will also determine how they perceive a particular situation. Someone who values safety will approach a situation checking for safety. A person who values excitement will have a different perspective on the same situation and will be willing to take risks outside of a comfort zone. You can see the internal struggle of choices based on core values. The average person makes thousands of choices a day, and each choice reflects some aspect of our value system. Once you have identified your core values, you can identify your purpose in life.

INFLUENCED UNAWARINGLY

Influence is a powerful thing. Sometimes we do things without knowing why. We could have been told, shown, or inspired. It has been estimated that as much as 77 percent of everything we think is negative and counterproductive and works against us. People who grow up in an average household hear "no" or are told what they can't do more than 148,000 times by the time they reach age eighteen.

A bride of several months was sawing away at the end of a ham. "Why," asked a neighbor, "are you sawing off the end of that ham?" "Because my mother always did it," the bride replied. A few days later, the neighbor met the bride's mother. "Your daughter tells me you always saw off the end of a ham before you bake it, and I wonder why." "Frankly," the mother replied, "I do it because my mother did it. Why not ask her?" The neighbor phoned the grandmother, who lived in the same town. The grandmother let her in on her secret. "I never owned a baking pan large enough to hold a ham. Why do you ask?" (Steve Shepherd) People do influence one another, good, bad, or otherwise. Many times, it turns into unintentional negative programming.

KEEP YOUR WINDSHIELD CLEAN

Have you ever noticed that you may not always look where you are going but you will always end up where you are looking? Perception is like looking through the windshield of a car. The mud of life and the sleet and hail of events can distract us. When we swerve and move outside the lines of protection, we take our sight off the road and could be headed for a serious crash. What we see from the inside is not always what is happening on the outside. A good windshield wiper can keep us focused. The wiper is on the outside, and so are many tools in life that help in the midst of a storm. Perception determines our choices and direction in life. Don't be locked inside your own view and opinion. Surround yourself with good wipers.

AN EXCUSE IS AN ESCAPE FROM RESPONSIBILITY

I recently caught myself giving an excuse for not being responsible for something I had committed to. The excuse was very truthful and validated a conflict in my schedule. It was a volunteer position that was dependent on my being there. I felt sick after I texted my supervisor that I couldn't make it. Not only did I leave him in a bind to find a replacement; it left a position empty that needed to be filled. I am a sixty-year-old man who should know better. What I had to face was that I had overcommitted. Learning to say no has always been a difficult thing for me to do. In the midst of endless demands, I often find myself making unwise decisions. I put the brakes on my volunteer commitment because I found myself forecasting excuses down the road as I looked at my calendar. Excuses are a *great* warning sign that something needs to change. I need to buy in or check out. If you find yourself making excuses, stop the engine and realize the importance of being responsible. An excuse is an escape from responsibility.

TURNING A BAD ENDING INTO A NEW BEGINNING

Have you ever been lost between the past you know and the future you don't know? There is so much pain and confusion in handling losses like those of a parent, a child, a marriage, a job, a reputation, health, and finances. Grief is a natural reaction to loss. Buried grief is unfinished business that rears its head in depression, anxiety, PTSD, and other ways. Completed grief allows us to remember the past and helps build the future. Allow grief to complete itself through different stages. The following are a few of many stages.

- Shock: "This can't be happening."
- Anger: "It's not fair, I don't deserve this."
- Bargaining: "I'll do anything to change this."
- Depression: "There's nothing worth living for."
- Acceptance: "I have to try again."

Faith transforms every ending into a new beginning.

SOMETIMES A LITTLE PUSH IS ALL I NEED

I remember learning how to ride a bike and how scared I was. Dad would start walking beside me, holding on to the seat. Soon his walk turned into a jog. He stayed beside me as I pedaled intently while looking forward. Then I looked to the side to see that he wasn't with me and I was on my own. What a great day that was when I learned to ride my bike. I couldn't have done it without a little push. Every year in Decorah, Iowa, baby eagles are filmed from the time they are hatched to the time they leave the nest. As the mama eagle nurtures and feeds them, they grow to the point when they are pushed out of the nest for the first time so they can learn to fly. As David McNally said, "Even eagles need a push." Learning to move outside my comfort zone has never been easy, and there are times when I needed a helping hand. Look for opportunities to walk beside and care for the ones you love. I am here today because of caring people around me who have given me a push. Sometimes a little push is all I need.

AN EXAMINED LIFE IS WORTH LIVING

Every day we wake up, we look into a mirror to see if we are presentable for the day ahead. We comb our hair, brush our teeth, and make sure our clothes and shoes match. We can spend hours "painting the barn" and forget what is on the inside. Self-evaluation and prepping for the day are critical for a positive outcome. How we look on the inside will determine how we act on the outside. There is not enough makeup in the world to cover up what is really going on. The truth will eventually work its way to the surface. Self-examination with a magnifying mirror allows us to reflect on the things that can help us and change us for the good. "Search me, God, and know my heart; test me and know my anxious thoughts. See if there is any offensive way in me, and lead me in the way everlasting" (Ps. 139:23–24). This a great Bible verse to memorize and to use every day with our internal mirrors. An examined life is worth living.

SOMEONE ELSE

We are all saddened to learn this week of the death of one of our most valuable associates, Someone Else. Someone's passing created a vacancy that will be difficult to fill. Someone has been with us for many years, and for every one of those years, Someone did far more than a normal person's share of the work. Whenever leadership was mentioned, this wonderful person was looked to for inspiration as well as results: "Someone Else can work with that group." Whenever there was a job to do, an extra hand needed, or a meeting to attend, one name was on everyone's lists—Someone Else! "Let Someone Else do it" was a common refrain heard throughout the company. It was common knowledge that Someone Else had one of the biggest hearts. Whenever there was a financial need, everyone just assumed Someone Else would pitch in and make up the difference. Someone Else was a wonderful person, sometimes appearing superhuman; but a person can only do so much. Were the truth known, everybody expected too much of Someone Else. Now Someone Else is gone! We wonder what we are going to do. Someone Else left a wonderful example to follow, but who is going to follow it? Who is going to do the things Someone Else did? Remember, we can't depend on Someone Else anymore!

BE AN OLYMPIAN—TRAIN

When our family was glued to the Olympics, rooting on the world's top athletes, I was inspired by their individual stories and commitment that prepared these athletes to do their best as they competed. But what was even more compelling than the highest ski jump, the elegant figure skating, the fastest bobsled, and the flare and flash of snowboarding was the Olympic spirit that ran in their veins. The timeless wisdom of the Bible offers five core values that these athletes *train* with. May we all incorporate these values into our personal lives as we continue to develop the kingdom Olympic warrior that we are called to be. The Olympics are full of teachable moments, and the Bible is full of character training.

- **Triumph:** Approach both success and failure gracefully.
- **Respect:** Treat others as you would have them treat you.
- **Alliance:** As iron sharpens iron, so a friend sharpens a friend.
- **Instinct:** Drive for excellence.
- **Never:** Never, never give up.

FOLLOW YOUR HEART

The path of passion is fueled by the beat of the heart. We are each uniquely created and designed for a purpose. "If a man does not keep pace with his companions, perhaps it is because he hears a different drummer. Let him step to the music which he hears, however measured or far away" (Henry Thoreau). The beauty of each heart is in the power of its beat. Listen to the desires of your heart, identify what you love to do, and begin pursuing it. When I graduated from college, I got hired for an elite position serving the west region as a sales consultant. The benefits were great, and the money was more than I could have ever imagined. But I was miserable because it didn't line up with the passions of my heart. After six months, I went into the regional manager's office, dropped the keys to my new company car on his desk, and told him I couldn't do the job. He offered me a substantial raise to stay, and I told him it wasn't about the money; it was about the passions of my heart. I made a choice at a young age to stay true to my heart's desire of helping people get to a better place. Thirty-five years later, I am true to my heart, which has fueled the passion of my life, in following the path that has been powerfully carved for me. Start with small steps and stay true to your heart's desires. You will notice an increase in your vitality, awareness, and purpose.

LESSON FROM HAWAII

For those of you who have had the privilege of visiting the volcanic island of Hawaii, you may have noticed an interesting phenomenon. On one side of the island is dark lava and, in some cases, hot flowing lava. It is barren and nonnegotiable for travel. There are boundaries that prohibit visitors. There is no plant growth, and the terrain is sharp and rigid. I have walked on hot rocks that have burned through the soles of my shoes. On the other side of the island is paradise with oceanfront properties, crystal beaches, and tropical gardens that provide shade, nourishment, and sacred pools with waterfalls. The same volcano has two sides to it, just as the voices and choices of life do. Likewise, there are two barks that are competing for our thoughts and actions. The soft, comforting bark is that of the good wolf. The loud, threatening bark is the bad wolf. The wolf that wins is the wolf we feed. Guiding our thoughts and navigating our days could make the difference between paradise and hell. What bark are you listening to?

UP ANCHOR

Have you ever met people who live in their past? Everything they do or think about doing is anchored in something they have done or that has happened to them. The first time I went to a high school reunion, I was shocked to see how many people were still living in their high school heads and body suits. The second time I went to a high school reunion, I left and have never been back. Memories can be anchors if we live in them instead of learning from them. "Forget the former things; do not dwell on the past. See, I am doing a new thing! Now it springs up; do you not perceive it? I am making a way in the wilderness and streams in the wasteland" (Isa. 43:18–19). I love the picture that Isaiah presents as our dreams catapult us into something new. The potential for something bigger and better springs up within us when our dreams become greater than our memories. The only way our dreams will ever come true is if we wake up. It's time to up anchor.

CAREGIVING IS A QUIET REWARD

Caregiving is way of life that is its own reward in simple, quiet ways. My dad had cancer during his last two years. I cared for him and watched his physical being wither away until his last breath. Some of my lasting memories are of him standing on the curb waiting for me to show up. He would drag his oxygen tank behind him and stand pointing his finger for me to park the car and get my a-- inside. We played 12,642 hands of gin rummy. As soon as I caught up with him, I refused to play anymore, as we ended in a tie—6,321 wins a piece. As death came over him, I watched every inch of his body turn cold until the last warm spot over his heart. That's the way he lived. Every action and deed came from his warm heart. Caregiving is the most difficult and yet most rewarding gift in walking beside our loved ones. June 20 will always be a special day as that is when I was rewarded with my dad's last earthly breath. For those of you who are caregivers, keep giving. For those of us who are transitioning forward, keep living. Those who have passed before us will live beyond us. Never lose hope and faith as they are secured in the love of our passed loved ones.

BALANCING EMOTIONS

A 2015 Disney film, *Inside Out*, did a wonderful job of teaching the importance of understanding and walking beside our emotions. The characters identified in the movie were Anger, Disgust, Fear, Joy, and Sadness. If we add a few more basic emotional characters, such as Love, Grief, and Greed, we will have a good picture of the main emotions that drive us. My favorite scene in the movie was when Joy and Sadness held each other's hands. One of the most difficult things for all of us to learn is how to walk beside and balance our emotions. It is important to know that an emotion is a temporary experience with positive or negative qualities. We must learn to embrace our emotions rather than be controlled by them. Here are a few tools to help you balance your emotions and gain control over them. Make a decision to nurture positive mental states such as compassion and kindness. Be proactive about moving beyond toxic emotions like anger, hatred, jealousy, and greed. Take responsibility for your emotions. Shifting blame takes away the ability to balance. Step back and put things into proper perspective instead of focusing on a perceived injustice. This may keep you from mislabeling a situation or problem and feeling upset over it. We all need a little help in managing versus being managed by our emotions.

ATTITUDES CHANGE THE COURSE OF LIFE

Attitude is one of the first things people tune in to in making an assumption. The best attitude quote I have ever read is from Charles R. Swindoll.

> The longer I live, the more I realize the impact of attitude on life. Attitude, to me, is more important than facts. It is more important than the past, than education, than money, than circumstances, than failures, than successes, than what other people think or say or do. It is more important than appearance, giftedness, or skill. It will make or break a company … a church … a home. The remarkable thing is we have a choice every day regarding the attitude we will embrace for that day. We cannot change our past.… We cannot change the fact that people will act in a certain way. We cannot change the inevitable. The only thing we can do is play on the one string we have, and that is our attitude.… I am convinced that life is 10 percent what happens to me and 90 percent how I react to it. And so it is with you.… We are in charge of our attitudes.

FLAT TIRE

I have coached kids for the past thirty years and have noticed a sinkhole on every team. If one kid has a bad attitude, the whole team suffers. Everyone in the dugout, bench, or sidelines sinks when a player starts heading in a downward spiral. I have tried leaving the troubled kids alone, getting in their faces, and benching them. It is a very tough circumstance because everyone on the team is watching or following. "A bad attitude is like a flat tire. You can't get very far until you change it," says Noah Coad. This quote sums it up very well. In changing a flat tire, you must jack the car up so that the pressure of the flat tire comes off the ground. The lug nuts must be loosened and the tire removed. Then and only then can a flat tire be fixed. So this is what I can learn about dealing with a sour disposition. I must do my best to relieve the pressure of the moment and begin to loosen the things that have made the person so tight. As the tension begins to loosen, I can then assist in removing the attitude and replacing it with a new one.

LEARNING TO
TRUST AGAIN—PART ONE

Trust can be broken, like a hammer shattering a glass table. Physical, emotional, sexual, and spiritual abuse can destroy a relationship and undermine a person's sense of security, safety, and well-being. Death, injuries, and trauma can also break the bonds of trust. And yet virtually every interaction in our lives is based on trust. We trust cars to start when we turn the ignition. We trust doctors to diagnose our symptoms. We trust banks to keep our money safe. We trust schools to provide an education. We trust our spouses to honor their marital vows. People whose trust has been destroyed can feel desperate and lonely as they perceive any interaction as a threat. Rebuilding trust is not only essential; it is foundational for healthy relationships. Trust is the glue that holds us together in difficult situations. In order to learn to trust again, *believe your future is different from your past.* This is very difficult to understand at first. If you focus on the rearview and side-view mirrors, this could prevent you from looking and believing that there is someone to trust through the windshield ahead. When there's a pattern of behavior or a situation that keeps repeating itself, it's important to use the past to guide you and not control you.

LEARNING TO TRUST AGAIN—PART TWO

Trust is the backbone and foundation of healthy, surviving relationships. When trust is broken, it is important to understand that rebuilding it is critical for survival. Trust is the glue that holds us together through trying times and difficult experiences. Here are some guides to learning to trust again:

- **Identify your beliefs and core values**. Whatever you believe in, you will become. You will attract the people in your life based on your own beliefs and values. Your beliefs can carry you forward in the bleakest of times. Identifying your core values can help predict your future. If you haven't identified your passions and the things that drive you, this would be a good time. They will help allow you to trust again.

- **Trust yourself again**. Believe and know that you are a good person! When you find it hard to trust others, it is often because you don't trust yourself. Not trusting your own judgments and decisions usually stems from a pattern of being wrong over and over. It is impossible to trust someone else if the trust is not embedded in you. This could lead to a vicious cycle of failed relationships. The only way off the hamster wheel of distrust is to trust, and it begins with you.

LEARNING TO
TRUST AGAIN—PART THREE

The reality of the life you live is that people you love and trust will let you down. Even with all the pain you are carrying from past brokenness, you can learn to trust again. So far we have talked about believing your future is different from your past, identifying your personal beliefs, and trusting yourself. Here are a few more insights in learning to trust again:

- **Take care of yourself.** A normal reaction to broken trust is withdrawing from relational interaction. Part of getting wind back in your sails is to look after yourself and understand that even though something happened to you, you can recover. Taking care of yourself will allow you to cope on your own. Self-care will give you confidence and make you feel better. There's something very powerful about doing something for yourself even when you don't want to.
- **Trust in God.** There is something authoritative and comforting about trusting in someone bigger than yourself and others. "Trust in the LORD with all your heart and lean not on your own understanding; in all your ways submit to him, and he will make your paths straight" (Prov. 3:5–6). God is and always will be true to His Word. You can count on Him to lead you with wisdom, peace, and strength. Not only is God trustworthy, but He will teach you to trust again.

UNLOCK YOUR MIND

Abraham Lincoln said, "All that we are is a result of what we have thought." We create our own worlds through our thoughts. Think about the clothes we wear, the chairs we sit in, and the houses we sleep in. Before these objects took their shape, they were thoughts. Think of the computers we use and the phones we are attached to. They were all created through ideas and transformed into products. Likewise, we create our own little worlds through the power of our thoughts. We are the writers, the directors, and the stars of our own life movies. One of my favorite scriptures is recorded in Ephesians 12:2: "Do not conform to the pattern of this world, but be transformed by the renewing of your mind." One of the greatest accomplishments we can achieve is breaking away from the patterns of the world and becoming the people we are supposed to be. It is up to us to protect what comes into and what comes out of our minds. There is plenty of negativity that would like to take up residence in our minds. Guard your mind and your thoughts and allow only the positive to find a home.

UNLEASH THE PS: PASSION, PURPOSE, PATH

It was recorded that a young boy asked Michelangelo why he was working so hard at chipping a block of marble that would become his greatest masterpiece, *David*. His reply was, "There's an angel inside this rock, and I'm setting him free." Life and its lessons chip away at us to create the divine masterpiece we are meant to be. This journey unleashes passion, purpose, and a path.

- **Passion** allows you to wake up in the morning with a leap out of bed and great anticipation. It is something you believe in and can't wait to get after. Passion is bigger than you are as you live within it.
- **Purpose** is like watching the trailer of your life movie for the day, week, and year. If you don't show up, you will miss out on the best scenes of your life. Purpose allows you to stay focused as you become aware of the distractions around you.
- A **path** is what weeds out the garden trail of your life. A path simplifies decision making as you look to move forward while allowing unwanted plant life to bring caution. A path that is laid with your passion and purpose will guide you and lead you to your destiny.

Unleash the Ps:

June 29

SPEAK INTO MY LIFE

I was in school away from home when I made an unpopular decision. I quit school and moved back home, telling my parents that I wanted to pursue a different course. I wanted to travel the country doing Christian concerts and recording. My parents were not pleased with me, but they allowed me to stay in the house while coaching me to finish school. It was a frustrating environment as I would stay in my room and practice singing and writing. Two weeks into my new pursuit, there came a knock on the door. A friend of mine had driven hours overnight to have a conversation with me. He said he couldn't sleep until he delivered a message to me. The message was very loud and clear: "Finish what you started and come back to school." These were the same words my parents had schooled me with. This was a divine meeting; I was hearing from someone else that I had made a mistake. I put my tail between my legs and went back to finish school. Since then I have completed a bachelor's, a master's, and a doctorate degree. I share this with you to highlight the importance of accepting and growing from your mistakes and being open to someone speaking into your life. I heard, listened, and responded to a voice much bigger than mine. Thank you, God!

BENEFITS
OF A CLOSE FRIEND

Inviting someone into your inner circle is not an easy thing to do. Most of us have been burned at some point in life. Studies have shown that close friendships can have a major impact on our health and well-being. Understanding the benefits of a friend can lead to having a friend. "A friend is someone who knows the song in your heart and can sing it back to you when you have forgotten the words" (Anonymous). Here are some benefits of having a friend:

- Increases your sense of belonging and purpose
- Helps you cope with traumas, such as divorce, serious illness, job loss, or the death of a loved one
- Prevents loneliness with needed companionship
- Boosts your happiness
- Reduces stress
- Improves your self-worth
- Encourages you to change or avoid unhealthy lifestyle habits

STOP, LISTEN, ABSORB, AND ACT

A wise but anonymous poet wrote the following words.

> If you can start the day without caffeine: if you can get going without pep pills; if you can always be cheerful, ignoring the aches and pains; if you can resist complaining and boring people with your troubles; if you can eat the same food every day and be grateful for it; if you can understand when your loved ones are too busy to give you any time; if you can forgive a friend's lack of consideration; if you can overlook it when those you love take it out on you, when, through no fault of your own, something goes wrong; if you can take criticism and blame without resentment; if you can ignore a friend's limited education and never correct him; if you can resist treating a rich friend better than a poor friend; if you can face the world without lies and deceit; if you can conquer tension without medical assistance; if you can relax without liquor; if you can sleep without the aid of drugs; if you can honestly say that deep in your heart you have no prejudice against creed or color, religion or politics; then you my friend, are almost as good as your dog.

This poem is dedicated to two kinds of people: 1) animal lovers, and 2) those who can stop, listen, absorb, and act. "Be alert and of sober mind, love each other deeply, and use your gifts to serve others" (1 Peter 4:1–2).

WHAT IF?

Some of the most difficult things to accept are the unknowns that have contributed to the loss of a loved one. All the *if onlys*, *what ifs*, *if I could haves*, and *I should haves* can haunt us and consume our thoughts. We can't get the unknown factors out of our heads as we constantly replay scenarios, trying to resolve and solve the unknown. The worst thing we can hear from someone is, "There's nothing you can do. Get over it!" I want you to picture the unknown as a big bad wolf growling and wanting to control you. There are three ways to face the wolf. One is to fight it face to face in a heated and consuming exchange of energy that leads to pure exhaustion. The second is to try to run from the wolf. The result of this is that there is nowhere to hide as we are constantly being followed and hunted. We live in fear of the attacks and are completely exhausted. The third is to acknowledge the presence of the wolf. The resolution here is to accept its awful presence without engaging in a heated battle or trying to run from its power. This is when we walk beside it, saying, "I feel you, I hear you, and I see you. You are not going to eat me or hunt me down. I will walk beside you until the growl goes away. I will learn to live with you."

WHAT'S BEHIND THE FLAG?—PART ONE

The national flag of the United States is often referred to as the American flag. It consists of thirteen equal horizontal stripes of red (top and bottom) alternating with white, with a blue rectangle in the canton (referred to specifically as the union) bearing fifty small, white, five-pointed stars arranged in nine offset horizontal rows—rows of six stars (top and bottom) alternate with rows of five stars. The fifty stars on the flag represent the fifty states of the United States of America, and the thirteen stripes represent the thirteen British colonies that declared independence from the Kingdom of Great Britain and became the first states in the new country (Wikipedia). There is so much symbolism and history in the flag.

When a flag is folded, it must be done a certain way because each of the thirteen folds holds its own meaning.

- The first fold of our flag is a symbol of life.
- The second fold is a symbol of the belief in eternal life.
- The third fold is made in honor and remembrance of the veterans departing our ranks who gave a portion of their lives for the defense of our country to attain peace throughout the world.

CollinsFlags.com

WHAT'S BEHIND
THE FLAG?—PART TWO

- The fourth fold represents our weaker nature, for as American citizens, it is to Him we turn in times of peace as well as in times of war for His divine guidance.
- The fifth fold is a tribute to our country, for in the words of Stephen Decatur, "Our Country, in dealing with other countries may she always be right; but it is still our country, right or wrong."
- The sixth fold is for where our hearts lie. It is with our hearts that we "pledge allegiance to the flag of the United States of America and to the republic for which it stands, one nation under God, indivisible, with liberty and justice for all."
- The seventh fold is a tribute to our armed forces, for it is through the armed forces that we protect our country and our flag against all of her enemies, whether they be found within or without the boundaries of our republic.
- The eighth fold is a tribute to the one who entered into the valley of the shadow of death that we might see the light of day, and to honor our mothers, for whom it flies on Mother's Day.

CollinsFlags.com

WHAT'S BEHIND THE FLAG?—PART THREE

- The ninth fold is a tribute to womanhood, for it has been through women's faith, their love, loyalty, and devotion that the character of the men and women who have made this country great has been molded.
- The tenth fold is a tribute to the father, for he, too, has given his sons and daughters for the defense of our country since they were first born.
- The eleventh fold, in the eyes of a Hebrew citizen, represents the lower portion of the seal of King David and King Solomon and glorifies in their eyes the God of Abraham, Isaac, and Jacob.
- The twelfth fold, in the eyes of a Christian citizen, represents an emblem of eternity and glorifies in their eyes God the Father, the Son, and Holy Spirit.
- As for the thirteenth fold, when the flag is completely folded, the stars are uppermost, reminding us of our nation's motto, "In God We Trust."

After the flag is completely folded and tucked in, it takes on the appearance of a cocked hat, ever reminding us of the soldiers who served under General George Washington and the sailors and marines who served under Captain John Paul Jones, who were followed by their comrades and shipmates in the armed forces of the United States, preserving for us the rights, privileges, and freedoms we enjoy today.

BIG EARS ARE BETTER THAN A BIG MOUTH

Have you ever wondered why we each have two ears and one mouth? We might be born with the ability to hear, but we must learn how to listen. If we increase our intake and decrease our output, we can learn when, where, and how to be effective listeners. Effective listening is not easy. It takes concentration and energy. The following are a few hints to help us become active listeners.

- **Respect:** Regard the speaker as worthy of your attention.
- **Stay focused:** It is so easy to let your mind wander and not be present.
- **Ask questions:** This allows clarification for both the sender and the receiver.
- **Give feedback:** Paraphrasing in your own words assures understanding.

GET RID
OF THE ROOSTER

Every morning of his young life, Booker T. Washington and his fellow slaves were awakened by the unwelcomed noise of a rooster. Long before the sun rose, the loud crow would fill the shanties, reminding the slaves to crawl out of bed and leave for the cotton fields. That rooster's crow came to symbolize a life of long, backbreaking days of labor. When Abraham Lincoln pronounced freedom with the Emancipation Proclamation, Booker was awakened again for the last time by a hysterical cry. This time, Booker's mom was chasing the rooster with an ax. That day, the Washington family fried and ate their haunting alarm clock for lunch. Their first act of freedom was to end the reminder that held them hostage. Are any "roosters" holding you hostage? You might need try sharpening the blade, or in the words of Paul, "forgetting those things which are behind and reaching forward to those things which are ahead" (Phil. 3:13).

WHAT DOES YOUR CHECKBOOK TELL?

If you want to evaluate your goals and priorities, look at your checkbook. How we spend our money and what we spend it on will magnify the heart connections in our lives. "For where your treasure is, there your heart will be also" (Matt. 6:21). So much in life is connected to money and our choices with it. We can learn a lot about ourselves and others by examining our spending habits. What I spend for food and consumption will determine the priority I place on health and its benefits. What I tithe to church and nonprofit organizations will tell if I am committed to my beliefs. What I spend for recreation will tell what my passions are. Our spending patterns speak louder than any words. Finances are the number-one cause of relational dysfunction. Poor choices in spending lead to divorce, addictive habits, communication breakdowns, deception, and mistrust. If you ever want to know the path that you're headed down, look at your checkbook. It's a great wake-up call if there needs to be change in your behaviors, and it is a great tool to authenticate the positive directions you are taking. What does your checkbook tell?

SURVIVING IN THE WAKE

The wake effect of a traumatic event reaches farther than we could ever imagine. The immediate consequences can be excruciating and overwhelming. The wake that is left behind an unfortunate circumstance is devastating. Some of the things that are sinking in the wake are loss of income, loss of identity, loss of hope, loss of dreams, loss of confidence, loss of faith, loss of confidence, loss of security, loss of friends, and loss of love. Learning to breathe in the wake of devastation is the only way to survive. Though there may not be an escape, there are life buoys you can hold on to while drifting in the waves. These life supports in your loss can be the only thing to grasp while sinking. Some of these supports could be someone who understands and is willing to listen without judging, family members who can be there in the deepest waters, friends who can put themselves aside, clergy who can hold your hand in offering spiritual comfort and assurance, counselors who identify with your loss, support groups that offer comfort with knowledge that another person is experiencing similar emotions, and journeying, which can be helpful as you write and get out. As difficult as your journey is, hold on to the life preservers so you can survive in the wake.

STRENGTHENING YOUR CORE

Identifying your core values will lead to a defined picture of the kind of person you want to be and the kind of life you want to have. The problem is that we can't get off the hamster wheel of life to get in touch with our core values. Too often we are controlled by external events and circumstances, which lead to a roller-coaster life of ups and downs. Our behaviors are then manipulated, controlled, and directed by the things that happen to us. Picture your heart as being the center of your core values. The integrity of the heart leads to the skillfulness of the hands. One can't survive without the other. Without a heart, your hands work aimlessly. Without your hands, a heart beats without action. Here are some things to help you learn about and identify your core values. They come from your character, your integrity, and your moral fiber. Explore these things to help define your values:

- What am I thinking about?
- What am I feeling?
- What am I communicating?
- What am I choosing?
- What are my behaviors?

HELP SOMEONE

There have been many times in my life when somebody walked beside me in difficult times. Whether it was life loss, property loss, or income loss, someone has showed up to comfort and guide me through the circumstance. I recently had someone walk beside me while I was pursuing a lifelong dream that was coming to fruition. I always wanted to write a book that could help people navigate the storms of life. Publishing a book is a journey of its own, with many winding roads. I hit a roadblock in this process that brought anxieties and doubt. A professional from the company realized the situation and immediately walked beside me to help me complete the dream of publishing my first book. Something that could have turned south was redirected to complete the book. As a result, *GPS: Your Guide through Personal Storms* has helped countless people in their lives. We all have speed bumps and potholes that can alter our desired course. People who have a core value of helping people will always have opportunities to help. I want to personally thank all the people in my lifetime who have helped me continue pursuing the passions of my heart. We need one another. If you haven't had the opportunity today, I encourage you to help someone. Your action could have a tremendous impact.

WHAT ARE YOU WAITING FOR?

The tragedy of life is not that we die but that we wait so long to live. I have helped many people transition in the dying process, and the most common theme I hear is, "I wish I had spent more time on the things that are important." The unfortunate pace of life is keeping us from the most important things in our lives. It is incredibly important to live each day as if it is your last. We all have an appointment with death. If we can treat each day as an opportunity to live rather than an obligation to live, our attitudes will change. The things that are most important in our lives will rise to the top instead of sinking underneath the hustle and bustle of the demands of a busy and hectic lifestyle. Make the changes you need to live. Our cemeteries are full of missed opportunities. Don't allow your life to be one of those that regrets a chance to do the right thing. Take the time to prioritize the most important things to you and begin to live for them. Connect with the passions of your heart and move toward them. What are you waiting for?

LEARNING TO SWIM IN GRIEF

Learning how to swim is a difficult process. The threat and fear of the unknown are conquered when we feel comfortable enough to put our faces and heads underwater. Life is like having our own personal swimming pools. We learn how to dog-paddle and tread water. We add different swimming strokes to make it through our yearly journeys. Out of nowhere, we get hit with traumatic life-changing events that drain our pools. The change and pain of our losses prevent us from refilling or revisiting the old pools because they will never be the same. We must learn how to swim in new pools. The problem is that we get pushed in—or we jump in—without learning how to swim again. We feel like we are drowning as we struggle to find new ways to survive. As it was when each of us learned how to swim in the first pool, we must feel comfortable enough to put our faces and heads in the water. There is no right way to wade into the water. It takes time and endurance for us to get used to the cold, along with moving toward the deep end. With patience and understanding, we can learn to swim in our grief.

BEYOND YOUR BOUNDARIES

A four-year-old was out riding her brand-new tricycle. Mom had to go inside for a few minutes but first had a stern conversation establishing the boundaries. She pointed to the neighbor's driveway on one side and a tree on their property on the other side. "You are to stay between the driveway and the tree. If you go past either, you will get a spanking." The child backed up her trike to her mom's feet and said, "You might as well spank me now. I have places to go." We all have places to go beyond the boundaries of our youth. You are created for a unique purpose in this life, and the only way to find out that purpose is to pedal beyond the safe zone. "Enlarge the place of your tent, stretch your tent curtains wide, do not hold back; lengthen your cords, strengthen your stakes. For you will spread out to the right and to the left" (Isa. 54:2–3). Keep pressing forward toward your God-given identity. Take an inventory of the passions that drive you. Those are the passions that drove our little four-year-old tricyclist. Don't allow the speed bumps, tight curves, potholes, and cracks in the sidewalk to keep you from pedaling. Don't let the driveways and trees prevent you from being who you were created to be. On your mark, get set, *go*!

GET OUT OF THE WAY

Have you ever learned that sometimes it is best to get out of the way or even disappear? When Dr. Mark Guy Pearse of England was in this country, he related an experience that presents a good lesson for all of us. He said he had been out fishing for trout; he had worked hard but caught none. His equipment was excellent, but he was unable to catch any fish. Finally, he came upon an old fisherman whose sack was full of trout. He asked him how he was so successful. The old fisherman answered, "There are three rules to follow in trout fishing: first, keep yourself out of sight; second, keep yourself further out of sight; third, keep yourself still further out of sight." As a parent, I have had to learn to step back and not be seen or heard in viewing the decisions my kids make. In coaching, I have had to teach myself to hide in the dugout or sidelines and let the kids play on their own. As a pastor, I have had to learn to let people make mistakes from a distance and allow God to transform them. As a counselor, I have had to get out of the way and let people make their own decisions. Sometimes the best results in life come from not being seen or heard.

MAKING IT REAL

Death Valley, the hottest place on the West Coast, is a desert floor that provides false hope and life in the form of a mirage. The more intense the heat gets, the more beautiful the mirage becomes. People today are chasing and putting their faith in false securities, turning over every rock along the way to try to find the secret. Some seek it through money and success; others pursue it in pleasure and success. The apostle John (1 John 1:1–7) unwrapped four guidelines that provide hope and purpose in making it real. The first is to secure the right foundation, the Word of Life. The second is to surround yourself with the right companions, having fellowship with one another. The third is to have the right source; God is light, and there is no darkness. And the fourth is to have the right goal—to walk in the light as He is in the light. So here is the groundwork for making it real: the right foundation, the right companions, the right source, and the right goal. How real is your life?

WHAT AM I LOOKING FOR?

We feed on the things on which our eyes are focused. Those things can be good for us or bad for us.

> Both the hummingbird and the vulture fly over our nation's deserts. All vultures see is rotting meat, because that is what they look for. They thrive on that diet. But hummingbirds ignore the smelly flesh of dead animals. Instead, they look for the colorful blossoms of desert plants. The vultures live on what was. They live on the past. They fill themselves with what is dead and gone. But hummingbirds live on what is. They seek new life. They fill themselves with freshness and life. Each bird finds what it is looking for. (Steve Goodier)

What I focus on will bring either life, hope, and strength or death, despair, and destruction. We get to choose!

TEAMWORK: 2 + 2 = 5

I grew up in a competitive home, married a competitive wife, and am parenting competitive kids. Competition is good if it drives us in a healthy way to get better. The downside is that some use it to dominate and lord over others in an unhealthy way. One of the things we have had to work on in our household is learning that we are all on the same team. This can be a challenge when you have teenage boys who live, eat, and breathe competition. Margaret Carty said, "The nice thing about teamwork is that you always have others on your side." Working together as a team allows us to challenge and complement each other. As a family, we can grow together more with one another's help. In our school lives, we can work together to get the assignments and homework done. On our sporting teams, we can work together to perform to our fullest potential. In the workplace, we can bring synergy to the team as we work together to accomplish the goals and mission of the company. Teamwork is something we should all strive for in every walk of life. There is great synergy in teamwork—greater than the sum we can reach on our own: 2 + 2 = 5

WHAT VOICE DRIVES ME?

There are two voices that are competing for your ears. Both have different roots, and both lead to different results. One voice is rooted in anger, pain, and jealousy. It is screaming injustice and recruiting people to stand and fight and to roam, kill, and destroy. This voice is getting louder and harder to shut out as crowds and armies are forming in our streets and along our borders. The result of this voice is death. The other is a small, still voice that is rooted in love, peace, and mercy. It is the voice of God through His Word that is calling us to seek Him and His righteousness. When we hear and respond to this voice, the result is a peace that surpasses all understanding and a life beyond what we see. The loud voice is recruiting those who are filled with rage, while the small, still voice is recruiting those who are filled with a hunger to know God. The choice is ours, and it depends on the desire for vengeance or the desire for mercy. Our choice determines the end result—life or death. "As for me and my house we will serve the Lord" (Joshua 24:15).

TEST YOUR FEELINGS

Feelings are wonderful things but not always trustworthy. They can give us insights into new and exciting situations. They can make us flutter with anticipation and allow our blood to reach the ends of capillaries we never knew existed. They can fill our minds and hearts with passion and direction. Our feelings allow us to draw closer to one another and to God. But the reality is that feelings are subjective. We can't always trust them. An event or situation can trigger a reaction to old feelings. Sometimes when old feelings creep back in, we feel fearful, ashamed, unloved, hopeless, angry, inadequate, helpless, resentful, bitter, victimized, and vengeful. I know this list can go on and on. A bad ending to a relationship, conflict on the job or at home, change, stress from a traumatic event, or disease and sickness can all ignite our feelings. Sometimes these feelings can come out of nowhere at any time. We could have disastrous results if we relied solely on the things we feel, see, and hear. We are not defined by our feelings. We are defined by our heads, hearts, and hands all being aligned. Always test your feelings before reacting. Allow yourself to be cautious with your past experiences and the counsel of those you trust.

TAKE COURAGE

A soldier in one of the regular batteries of the Confederacy had displayed conspicuous bravery in a dozen engagements while serving with his gun as a cannoneer. At the Battle of Chickamauga, he was assigned the duty of driver. Instead of participating in the excitement of loading and firing, he could only sit quietly and watch the havoc created around him by the enemy's bullets. He soon became seized with fear that completely unmanned him. His courage leaked away when he had nothing to do. There is a spiritual battle that is raging all around us, and because we do not have a sense of what our wartime assignment is, we lose heart and are filled with fear because we have become disengaged from the battle. Rather than finding the courage to declare victory within us, we find ourselves sinking in the battle that rages around us. We become filled with fear, anxiety, and disillusionment at our own ability to wage war on the enemy of our souls. "For the Lord your God is he who goes with you to fight for you against your enemies, to give you the victory" (Deut. 20:4).

WHAT'S THE BEST CHOICE?

Are you ever stuck or torn about a situation and don't know the right decision to make? The average person makes thirty-five thousand choices a day, and most of those are a result of previous choices. So the tough part is in making the right choice. How do we make the *best* choice? Paul wrote, "And this is my prayer: that your love may abound more and more in knowledge and depth of insight, so that you may be able to discern what is best and may be pure and blameless" (Phil. 1:9–10). If we are rooted and motivated in love and can wrap our minds around knowledge and insight, we will have the tools needed to make the right choice. The result of the best choice is knowing that we have done our best and can rest in it.

MAKE THINGS HAPPEN

A friend shared an illustration with me. "I realize that I need to be part of changing the country that I know best. But that's too big, so I will start with my town. But that's too big, so I will start with my street. That too is too big, so I will start with my family. No, that's too big, so I must begin with myself." I'm sure you want to make things happen. There are three kinds of people in the world: people who *make* things happen, people who *watch* what's happening, and people who *wonder* what happened. We have a choice in life to make, watch, or wonder. People who watch will be on the sidelines wishing they could get in on the action. People who wonder will have thoughts that ruminate and bounce around like a wayward ball. They will wonder what happened and what they missed. People who make things happen will always be in the mix of things and part of a purpose. Knowing that we are part of something much bigger than what we thought and what we expected is fulfilling and meaningful. What kind of a person are you? It's time to make things happen.

GARAGE SALE

This is the time of year when so many of us clear our houses of stuff that has accumulated over time. It feels so good to get rid of it all so we can have more space that was once held captive by useless "stuff." We do the same thing with thoughts, habits, negative attitudes, fears, time zappers, and distractions, which fill our minds and hold us hostage to the junk from our past. Some of the things we need to take to the curb are feelings of insecurity, loneliness, neglect, the need to please everyone, living in past failures, jumping to negative conclusions, the fear of looking foolish, and anything else we don't want to pass on to our kids. Paul teaches us to "no longer conform to the patterns of the world but be transformed by the renewing of your mind" (Rom. 12:2). The best garage sale we could ever have is one in which we get rid of the old, unwanted debris from our minds and replace it with a new attitude that refreshes our minds.

SUCCESS COMES FROM FAILURE

Failure is a teaching tool. The greater the failure is, the greater the opportunity to learn and grow is. Once we realize that our mistakes are a chance to cultivate even greater outcomes and results than we anticipated, we can absorb and produce because of them. Thomas Edison said, "I'm not discouraged, because every wrong attempt discarded is another step forward." He became a full-time inventor at the age of twenty-one and set up his own laboratory. He and his team would have as many as forty ongoing projects at one time. Edison applied for more than four hundred patents a year. He struggled with many of his inventions. Failure after failure caused him to be determined and persistent in his passions. With his determined dedication and more than ten thousand experiments, he invented the incandescent light bulb in 1879. Despite all of his misfortunes, he said, "I haven't failed. I've found ten thousand ways that don't work." Success comes from failure. Be persistent and never give up on your passion and desires. Believe and trust in the gifts and talents that God has given you. Keep moving and have faith in what lies ahead of you.

WE ARE CREATED FOR ONE ANOTHER

We are created to be in relationships. We each came into this life with an umbilical cord connecting us to our mom. Not only are we created to exist with one another, but we are created to interact with one another. Everything in life is done through relationships. Our conflicts, our teamwork, our cooperative efforts, and our group relationships are essential for our growth. Family structures, classrooms, sporting teams, coworkers, churches, and clubs help us to understand the importance of relational survival. My three favorite words in life (*hope, faith,* and *love*) demonstrate the power of relationships. With hope, we believe together. With faith, we grieve together. With love, we exist together. Hoping together gives us the ability to see beyond the existing circumstances. We can embrace one another and believe together. Having faith together allows us to grieve knowing that we can move together toward the things beyond our situations. Having love for one another allows us to coexist. Our love is the source of our lives. Without love, we would wither away with no reason to live. Almighty God has created us to live with one another. We must embrace hope, faith, and love to understand.

GOOD GRIEF!

Grief is defined as the emotions and distress following a loss. Grief can be caused by many different losses, such as death, sickness, loss of a job, divorce or breakup, move, or a change in lifestyle. Everyone experiences grief a little differently. Psychiatrist Elisabeth Kubler-Ross identified five main stages of the grief process. These are just a few of many different stages.

- **Denial:** This is the shock reaction. "It can't be true." "No, not me." We refuse to believe what happened.
- **Anger:** Resentment grows. "Why me?" "Why my child?" "This isn't fair!" We direct blame toward God, others, and ourselves. We feel agitated, irritated, moody, and on edge.
- **Bargaining:** We try to make a deal, insisting that things be the way they used to be. "God, if you heal my little girl, then I'll never drink again." We call a temporary truce with God.
- **Depression:** Now we say, "Yes, me." The courage to admit our loss brings sadness (which can be healthy mourning and grieving) or hopelessness (which is unhealthy mourning and grieving).
- **Acceptance:** Now we face our loss calmly. It is a time of silent reflection and regrouping. "Life has to go on. How? What do I do now?"

THE BEST THING FOR YOU—PART ONE: LOOSENING YOUR GRIP

Have you ever gripped a chain-link fence so hard that the circulation to your fingers stopped, causing them to turn purple? The only cure is to let go. Studies have shown many benefits if we can learn to do two things—let go and *forgive*. Forgiveness can't change the past, but it can change the future. Here are some benefits of this healthy decision:

- Forgiveness is good for your heart. It is associated with lower heart rate and blood pressure as well as stress relief. This can bring long-term health benefits for your heart and overall health.
- Forgiveness is associated with five measures of health: physical symptoms, medications used, sleep quality, fatigue, and somatic complaints. The reduction of depressive symptoms strengthens spirituality, conflict management, and stress relief.
- Forgiveness releases the offending party, which allows positive behaviors toward others outside of the relationship.

Forgiveness is good for your body, your relationships, and your place in the world. Next we will look at some tools for how to forgive.

THE BEST THING FOR YOU—PART TWO: FORGIVENESS SHAKES OFF THE DIRT

A farmer's mule fell into a well. He had no way to get him out, so he decided to bury him there. He dumped a truckload of dirt on top of the mule. The mule started snorting and kicking until he worked his way to the top of the pile. Truckload after truckload of dirt, the mule kept shaking it off until the dirt reached the top and he walked out of the well. What was intended to bury him ended up helping him come out on top. No matter how bad a situation looks or feels, God will always provide a way out, and He will use the piles of dirt to mature and complete you. The key to coming out on top is to forgive the dirt and shake it off or you will get buried. Forgiveness can't change the past, but it can change the future. Shake it off and walk away.

THE BEST THING FOR YOU—PART THREE: MOVING FORWARD

Figuring out how to forgive can be very difficult, especially when you have been hurt. We have a tendency to hold on to things because we don't want to open the wound or revisit the pain. The misperception is that if we forgive, we are opening ourselves up to future repeats of the same negative treatment. The reality is that by holding on to the pain or offense, we are sleeping in the same prison cell with the offense that is tormenting us. These tools will be helpful in your journey to be free from the stress of the past.

- **Look for the positive:** Look for and focus on the benefits you have gotten from a negative situation.
- **Forgiveness is more for me:** People don't need to know that you've forgiven them, especially if they are no longer in your life.
- **Express yourself:** Write in a journal, letter, or card to release your emotions. Confide in a counselor or friend.

WE CAN CHOOSE THE ACTION BUT NOT THE RESULTS

Everything we do has a result connected to it. We should all strive for positive results in our lives. The average adult makes thirty-five thousand choices a day, which validates the importance of making the right choice. What we choose to do will dictate the outcomes in our lives, both positive and negative.

1) Be prepared to make good decisions. The best way to anchor good choices is to stay connected and close to your core values. Your core values are your beliefs, passions, and morals. Your core values will provide a filter for the decision-making process.

2) Evaluate the outcomes, benefits, and consequences of your choices. If we can slow down enough in our choosing, we can predict what the future holds. Look ahead in your choices to see the projected outcomes.

3) Follow through and don't be afraid. Sometimes the consequences of our choices can be corrected if we follow through with doing the right thing. Too often we suffer because of something we didn't do. Listen to your thoughts and let your heart guide you. Trust the feedback from resources like your education, friends, and family. Personal knowledge and experience will guide you.

Being prepared, looking ahead to the outcomes, and following through with good choices will help predict the outcomes of your life.

GROWTH SPURTS

Growth spurts are a part of life that we all must go through. There are three certain elements that contribute to our emotional growth—relationships, discipline, and experiences. Understanding the combination of these essentials and giving them our attention will keep us growing and reaching our fullest potential.

- **Relationships:** We are birthed in relationship, and we continue to survive as a result of relationships. "As iron sharpens iron, so one man sharpens another" (Prov. 27:17). Being a member of the human race involves knowing difficult people along with those we relate to. How we learn to work with everyone helps sharpen us in our growth spurts.
- **Discipline.** Certain practices are vital to our growth. Learning from our mistakes and practicing discipline will keep us growing in a positive direction. Discipline has many faces that contribute to our spurts: solitude, mindfulness, eating, exercising, education, and faith. Discipline is like vitamin water to our growth.
- **Experiences:** Our experiences give us different perspectives on situations that cause us to think and act outside of our box. The things that have happened to us, both positive and negative, contribute to our growth. Love, suffering, pain, and joy are all teachers of our souls.

Our growth is determined by where we have been, where we are, and where we are going. Accept the growth spurts and mature with them.

THE BATTLE WITHIN—PART ONE

Have you ever been in a position or state of mind in which you felt trapped and ended up doing things that you didn't want to do? You knew those things were bad for you. You knew they would lead to anxieties and anxious thoughts. Your heart said, *Don't do it*, your head said, *Don't do it*, but you did it anyway. You wanted to stop, but you didn't know how. Before you can stop doing the things that you know aren't good, you must understand where the root of the action is. I want to uncover two different options that might be the root of your struggle. The first is fear. An acronym I find quite useful in defining fear is False Expectations Appearing Real. Your fears can control you and manipulate you into doing things that you don't want to do. One of these fears could be the fear of rejection. If you have a fear of rejection, you are setting yourself up to be rejected. Another fear might be not meeting expectations. If you feel like you're going to let somebody down (an associate, a friend, or a family member), you probably will. Another fear might be that you're not good at anything. No matter what you do, you always fail. So you have a fear of failure. These fears can keep you locked up in a box. Your fears predict your future if you live in them.

THE BATTLE WITHIN—PART TWO

The apostle Paul describes this battle within: "I obviously need help! I realize that I don't have what it takes. I can will it, but I can't do it. I decide to do good, but I don't really do it; I decide not to do bad, but then I do it anyway. My decisions, such as they are, don't result in actions. Something has gone wrong deep within me and gets the better of me every time" (Rom. 7:18–19). The second option I want to address that might be hindering your struggle within is a possible identity crisis. The difficulty with this option is that your identity comes from the things you hold on to and can't let go of. The rearview mirror provides insight to where you have been, while the windshield allows you to look forward to where you are going. Unfortunately, you can get stuck living in your past instead of letting your past catapult you into your future. Our identities are a constant transformation of becoming bigger and better because of what we've gained and learned. Our authentic identities come from the things we become through the things that we've done.

CHANGING
THE WHY TO HOW

Life is a roller coaster of ups and downs. Every valley and every mountaintop has a lesson for us, if we are teachable. I am accepting when it comes to my own difficulties. But when dealing with others' pain, I have a tendency to dwell on the *why*, which leads to anger, frustration, depression, anxiety, and so forth. I lose sleep, weight, hair, desire, hope, passion, patience, perseverance, and purpose. I build a case against God and against others. Why them and not someone else? Why them and not me? So for me to survive in someone else's pain along with my own, I have to switch to *how* rather than *why*. How can I love God more in this situation? I need to swim in the *how* to love Him more despite the horrible circumstances. Here are a few tools:

- **Accept:** "Father, if you are willing, take this cup from me; yet not my will, but yours be done" (Luke 22:42).
- **Be free:** "Out of my distress I called on the Lord; the Lord answered me and set me free" (Ps. 118:5).
- **Be in peace:** "Do not let your hearts be troubled and do not be afraid" (John 14:27).

The most difficult switch to make is from *why* to *how*.

AGAINST ALL ODDS

A very close friend of mine was diagnosed with colon cancer. Our family stood beside him and his family as he was fighting for his life. He lost one hundred pounds and was sinking fast in the grip of this horrible disease. Prayers, new treatments, and the faith of his family and friends brought him strength and courage. The spread of the cancer slowed down as he started getting his physical life back. Over the course of several months, he began putting weight back on and gaining strength. Today, he is cutting his grass and helping maintain the softball field that one of his kids plays on. The doctors say the cancer will never go away and that he will always be subject to the symptoms and care for the sickness. I have enjoyed the best fish fries in his garage, his lawn looks better than mine, and he has the best attitude. This man is teaching me how to live in the face of adversity. I'm not sure how many days, months, or years he has left in his earthly body suit, but I do know that he is paving a way for his family and friends to follow. His fight and ability to live each day as it might be his last has been a great example of faith. Thank you, Dave, for my life lesson on surviving against all odds.

BUILDING TRUST

Trust is at the core of every relationship. When trust is present, communication flows freely. When trust is broken, not so much. Most of us have been part of building trust and destroying trust, sometimes in the same relationship. Building trust is always the better choice and will always lead to healthy consequences. Trust builds bridges. Here are some helpful hints to become a trust builder:

- Admit your mistakes and grow from them. Mistakes are the number-one ingredient in growth.
- Be honest all the time, not just some of the time. Honesty is a character builder and the foundation of trust.
- Be true to your values and anchor in them. Our core values are the only things we have to keep us on track. They are the anchor when the winds of mistrust prevail.
- Be open and vulnerable in sharing and receiving information. Self-disclosure will build trust in every relationship.
- Be committed and clear in your convictions. Stay committed to your values and convictions. Your commitment will lead to building trust.

Do everything you can to be a trust builder in all of your relationships, whether in the home or in the business world.

WHAT'S ON THE OTHER SIDE OF THE SANDBAG?

Much of what we do day in and day out doesn't seem to matter until it becomes a paint stroke on the canvas of our lives. We can go through life filling sandbag after sandbag with the mundane effort of shoveling dirt. There is nothing glamorous about a shovel and a pile of dirt that wears us out physically and emotionally. If we can turn our labor into an act of love, our sandbags have new meaning. Every sandbag we fill becomes part of a dike that is much bigger than we ever thought it would be. What's on the other side of the sandbags are events and circumstances that can have devastating effects in our world. Mother Teresa wasn't motivated by fame or wealth. She was consumed with a passion to fill her sandbags by ministering to the unmet needs of the forgotten people in the slums of Calcutta. If we can embrace all of our efforts to help those around us, we can bring peace in chaos. We may never know what is on the other side of our sandbags, but what we need to know is that we all have the opportunity to make a difference. One of Mother Teresa's slogans was "A life not lived for others is a life not lived at all."

MY HEART CONDITION

If not detected in time, heart disease can kill a person physically, spiritually, and emotionally. Solomon wrote, "Above all else, guard your heart, for it is the wellspring of life" (Prov. 4:3). What are my thoughts anchored in? Am I constantly comparing, resenting, or envious? Am I easily angered? Am I stressed out twenty-four/seven? Am I positive or negative in speaking to or about others? Getting my heart right is critical for survival. If the water in my well is polluted, it will make me sick. If I keep drinking it, it will kill me. "Create a pure heart in me, O God, and put a new and loyal spirit in me" (Ps. 51:10). I must get to the heart of my problem, which is the problem of my heart. Here are three great words for me to coat my heart with immediately: *pure, new,* and *loyal*.

MANAGING THE FEAR OF THE UNKNOWN

Fear of the unknown is difficult to manage because we are fixing our thoughts and actions on something that is out of our control. When empowered, this fear can hinder our ability to think, feel, and act in ways that are normal for us. This fear can manifest itself in many forms: anxieties, isolation, panic, intrusive thoughts, excessive worries, terror, and horror, to name a few. Here are some things to help you manage the fear of the unknown:

- **Understand it:** Fear is a natural human instinct. There are three responses to fear: 1) wrestle and fight it, which leads to exhaustion; 2) run from it, which leads to being constantly chased; or 3) walk beside it. If we can walk beside fear, we will take its power away. Our fears will never go away, but understanding them is managing them.
- **Fix your eyes on something beyond:** Hope give us the vision to see beyond the circumstances. The visualization of something positive can help manage fear.
- **Educate yourself:** Find professional resources to guide you in your journey. Avoid self-diagnosis or internet solutions as they will add to your fear instead of managing it.

- **Take small steps forward:** Baby steps forward will help you manage your fear over a period of time. Use guide rails and walkers to assist you in moving forward.
- **Use humor:** Our minds tend to think about the worst-case scenarios, but the worst may not happen at all. Humor takes our minds off the unknown.

THE ART OF AN APOLOGY

If your actions have caused hurt feelings, anger, or deep-seated ill will, an apology is in order. Apologizing is not an acknowledgment of weakness. A *sincere* apology can have a tremendous amount of healing power for both the receiver and the giver.

An effective apology will communicate the three Rs: *regret, responsibility,* and *remedy.*

- **Regret:** Communicate the regret you feel sincerely. Even in cases where your intention was not to upset or hurt someone, the apology must come from your heart.
- **Responsibility:** Do not make excuses or blame others. Accept total responsibility for your actions. Don't say, "I'm sorry about what happened, but you shouldn't have …"
- **Remedy:** A meaningful apology should include a commitment to not repeat the behavior. It might also include an offer of restitution.

CALL IN THE TROOPS—PART ONE: SPIRITUAL WARFARE STRATEGY

God uses traumatic events to build our faith and secure our hope in Him. We are in a constant battle between good and evil. We have an opportunity to anchor our hearts, minds, souls, and strength in the blessed hope of eternal life with Him and fellow heirs to the kingdom. Personal experiences are meant to be shared as we encourage one another in our chase for God's purpose and understanding. We will need one another and the Holy Spirit to keep moving forward in the face of battle.

Spiritual Warfare Strategy

- **Call in the troops**. This is the time to use the army that God has provided in the spiritual warfare. "For the *weapons* of our *warfare* are not of the flesh but have divine power to destroy strongholds" (2 Corin. 10:4, emphasis added).
- **Prepare yourself.** Know that we are in a constant battle and we need to do everything we can to prepare ourselves for battle. "Therefore gird up the *loins of your mind,* be sober, and *rest your hope* fully upon the grace that is to be brought to you at the revelation of Jesus Christ" (1 Peter 1:13, emphasis added). "Love the Lord your God with all your heart and with all your soul and with all your strength and with all your mind" (Luke 10:27).

CALL IN THE TROOPS—PART TWO: SPIRITUAL WARFARE STRATEGY

- **Know your enemy.** The greatest victories we have seen through the course of history are a result of knowing who the enemy is. We must be aware of our enemy's tactics and beat him on his grounds.

Finally, be strong in the Lord and in his mighty power. Put on the full armor of God, so that you can take your stand against the devil's schemes. For our struggle is not against flesh and blood, but against the rulers, against the authorities, against the powers of this dark world and against the spiritual forces of evil in the heavenly realms. (Eph. 6:10–13)

- **Go into battle.** This is a battle we can't run from or avoid. We must go into the battle knowing that God is victorious. "The Lord your God, who is going before you, will *fight* for you" (Deut. 1:30, emphasis added). "Fight the good *fight* of the faith. Take hold of the eternal life to which you were called when you made your good confession in the presence of many witnesses" (1 Tim. 6:12, emphasis added).

STUCK BETWEEN CHOICES

I remember sitting at the dining room table with my dad. It was one of those memorable mentoring moments. He had a spoon and turned it over in his hand as he told me that everything has two sides to it. He then laid out ten playing cards on the table. Each card represented a choice and the results of that decision. What he taught me was to weigh my choices against other choices in making the best decision for myself. The playing cards were eliminated one at a time until there was one left. That last card helped me determine the best choice for the situation. As a counselor and pastor, I have used this teaching tool in helping people in their difficult choices. If we can learn to take the time and explore different outcomes, which include the ripple effect of the choices, we can help pave the road for a better tomorrow. Life is full of challenges that present themselves through our choices. If you feel stuck or don't know what to do, pull out a deck of cards and place a few of them in front of you. Each card will represent an option. Start the elimination process, and make the best choice. "Whatever you do, do all to the glory of God" (1 Corin. 10:31).

THE EMPTY CHAIR—PART ONE

A daughter asked a pastor to pray with her dad. When he arrived, the pastor found Joe lying in bed with his head propped up on two pillows and an empty chair beside his bed. "I guess you were expecting me," he said. "No, who are you?" the father asked. "Your daughter called me, and when I saw the empty chair, I figured you were expecting me." "The empty chair—" began the dad. "I've never told anyone this, not even my daughter. All of my life, I have never known how to pray. I used to hear about prayer, but it always went right over my head. Four years ago my best friend said to me, 'Joe, prayer is a simple matter of having a conversation with Jesus. Here's what I suggest. Sit down on a chair, place an empty chair in front of you, and in faith see Jesus on the chair.'"

THE EMPTY
CHAIR—PART TWO

Joe's friend had continued. "It's not spooky because he promised, 'I'll be with you always.' Then just speak to Him and listen in the same way you're doing with me right now." Joe paused. "So, I tried it and liked it so much that I do it a couple of hours every day. I'm careful, though. If my daughter saw me talking to an empty chair, she'd either have a nervous breakdown or send me off to the funny farm." Deeply moved, the pastor prayed and left. Two nights later, the daughter called the pastor with the news of her dad's passing. "Before I left the house, he called me over to his bedside, told me one of his corny jokes, and kissed me on the cheek. When I got back from the store an hour later, I found him dead. But there was something strange. In fact, it was beyond strange—kind of weird. Apparently, just before Daddy died, he leaned over and rested his head on the chair beside the bed."

WHO CONTROLS THE REMOTE?

The remote control is a powerful instrument in our house as it locks on to a desired channel. The remote is useless without batteries. We are in a constant spiritual battle for the batteries that control the remote. We are in conflict with the sinful nature of our earthly birth versus the spirit nature of our eternal birth in Christ. "The sinful nature wants to do evil, which is just the opposite of what the Spirit wants. And the Spirit gives us desires that are the opposite of what the sinful nature desires. These two forces are constantly fighting each other" (Gal. 5:17). So here lies the battle: When the batteries in the remote are our sinful nature, we lock onto channels of behavior that cause us to do things that benefit us, that turn into bad choices, such as addictions. When the batteries are of the Holy Spirit, we lock onto the channels of God that will benefit others. It might be time to get rid of the old batteries and replace them with new ones. That begins with Christ!

OPTIONS IN CONFLICT

How we choose to work through our differences will determine patterns we will use all our lives. Our responses have a lot to do with our personalities. Here are a few options we may choose in conflict situations:

- **"I'm going to get you."** This approach exemplifies an *I win; you lose* approach to conflict. It becomes my duty to show you. It's my way or no way. Things are black and white with no room for anything that is gray. This is a power method of resolving conflict.
- **"I'll get out."** When the heat is on, I am out of here. I am uncomfortable, so I'll withdraw. Conflicts are hopeless. People can't change, so what's the point? See ya!
- **"I'll give in."** I will yield to the conflict for the sake of the relationship. I am generous and submissive on the outside, but I'm tense and tight on the inside. I will become a doormat because the differences aren't worth struggling over. You win!
- **"I'll meet you halfway."** This is a creative compromise that allows both parties to meet in the middle of the conflict and usually requires some sacrifice by both parties. Compromising is a gift in sustaining relationships.
- **"I care enough to confront."** I will take an honest and considerate position. Conflict is neutral and meaningful, and we are able to work through it.

GOD LEADS, GOD FEEDS, AND GOD WEEDS

I remember being on the beach when I saw a lifeguard come running out of the tower and into the water. Sirens started sounding as he wrapped his arms around a kid and pulled him to safety. There had been a shark sighting, and everyone was ordered out of the water as it was declared unsafe to swim. Our loving God rescues us at times when we are cruising along and asking Him for things we think are important to us. When God says no, it is usually because there is a shark in the water and He has other plans. There have been countless times when, if God would have said yes, I would have married the wrong person, taken the wrong job, moved when I shouldn't have, made bad choices in ministry, and so on. The hardest lesson for me to learn is that when God says no, something is not good for me. When God says yes, something is good for me. God is like the lifeguard who sees things beyond our line of sight and rescues us from troubled waters that we aren't aware of. He does so simply with a yes or no to things we ask for and think are most important for us. He loves us so much that He says no. God leads, God feeds, and God weeds us if we let Him.

HANDLING FAILURE

Even the most seasoned people experience failure. The big question at such times shouldn't be, "How could I have let this happen?" but "What's the right way to deal with it?" Beating ourselves up is a natural reaction as we have ruminating, self-condemning thoughts. This does us no good as it produces discouragement, defeat, and despair. I recently experienced one of the worst failures of my life. I have been officiating funerals for thirty-seven years and spend significant time in preparing for each celebration of life. I have one chance to present the best service I can. But in this case, I addressed the surviving son of the deceased by the wrong name. I misnamed him a few times before someone in the audience stood up and yelled at me. I wanted to find the biggest rock to hide behind. Not only was I embarrassed, but the rest of the service was derailed as I couldn't focus. I had my first major complaint in thirty-seven years, and it wasn't pretty. My heart sags even writing about it. However, I can only learn from and use my mistake to make me better. When you fail, don't lie down and give up. Handle your failure by minimizing your downtime so you can get back up and walk again.

IF YOU WANT CHANGE, BECOME IT

I have found that the best way for me to make a difference is to become the difference. Whether parenting, coaching, pastoring, or counseling, the best action to create action is my own. I must remain passionate and willing to become the end result. Here are some tools that might help in overcoming the hurdles in making a difference:

- **Take decisive and immediate action:** It doesn't matter if you are a genius or highly educated, you can't change anything or make any sort of real-life progress without taking action. Knowledge and wisdom are both useless without action. There's a huge difference between knowing and doing.

- **Spend the time needed for change:** Never put off or give up on a goal that's important to you. Life is shorter than it sometimes seems. All we have is today as tomorrow may not come. Follow your heart and passion today.

- **Always be a student:** Experience, learn, and absorb all the knowledge you can. Prepare yourself for change by keeping your mind fresh with new opportunities to change. If you stay ready, you don't have to get ready.

- **Stop being afraid:** Instead of thinking about what could go wrong, think about what could go right.

THE GREATEST CELEBRATION IS ONE THAT NEVER ENDS

I have been part of and seen many celebrations over my lifetime. Some of my favorites are sports celebrations. Professional sports players have always had a unique flair for partying after a touchdown, a goal, a home run, a hole in one, a perfect game, a buzzer beater, and a checkered flag. Youth sports have captured their share with some memorable moments of the first hit, the first tackle, and the first fish. These celebrations are short lived and forgotten about. The greatest celebration I ever witnessed was when my dad passed in my arms. After being in a coma, his eyes opened and became as big as golf balls. I asked him, "Do you see heaven?" "Yes!" "Do you see angels?" "Yes!" "Do you see Jesus?" He said, "Yesss—" as he took his last breath. My dad showed me that the greatest celebration is one that never ends. His faith allowed him to see and experience life beyond the grave. The celebrations of things we see and accomplish in our earthly lives are nothing compared to the greatest celebration of life that never ends. And to that, I say thank you, Jesus, for your life, death, and resurrection.

CHECK YOUR TANK

Have you ever run out of gas and ended up on the side of the road? Newer cars today have warning lights and whistles that warn us when our fuel is low, and we still end up on the side of the road with an empty tank, forcing us to push for the extra mile. We do the same thing in the hamster wheels we run on in our daily lives. Our bodies will give us warning signs through physical and emotional stressors, but we keep going to get the extra mile. Our survival depends on knowing when to stop and fill our tanks. Look for the warning signs and get off the wheel of misfortune before you become another statistic. Know your body and pay attention to it when the low fuel light comes on. Do what you need to do to fill up. Everyone is different regarding self-care. We must do what is right. Here are some of the things I do physically, emotionally, and spiritually: sports, both watching and engaging in them; reading; watching recorded TV shows, because commercials take up fifteen minutes of an hour-long show; reading scriptures; and praying. Whatever you can do for yourself, do it so you don't run out of gas. Look for and listen to the signs of an empty tank.

GUIDE TO HEALING TRAUMA

I want to take time to identify a few things that can help you in healing any trauma that has happened in your life or in the lives of others you may know. Trauma survivors can incorporate these tools along with others in the recovery process.

- **Education:** Open yourself up to learning about the effects and nature of trauma. Awareness of trauma and its symptoms can help you identify concerns and guide you to self-care. Professional care is an option when we understand the seriousness of the impact of the trauma.
- **Listening:** Finding someone who listens provides comfort, acceptance, and nonjudgment. A good listener opens the window of hope.
- **Expressing emotions:** It is important to find a safe place to express anger, frustrations, fears, and anxieties relating to the trauma. Expressing the emotional impact of the experienced trauma is necessary for healing.
- **Boundaries:** Structuring boundaries will help protect the survivors from old, current, and future trauma. This includes relational trauma as well.

- **Positivity:** Focus on the positive strengths that can result from the healing of trauma. There is something positive to be gained from trauma if we search for it.
- **Forgiveness:** Survivors who can learn to forgive will open themselves up to healing. Unforgiveness holds us hostage to the trauma.

MANAGING THE PRESSURE COOKER

Water boils at 212 degrees Fahrenheit. No matter how long it continues to boil, it always stays the same temperature. As the water evaporates and becomes steam, it is also the same temperature—212 degrees. The only way to make the steam and water hotter is to put them under pressure. If we fit an absolutely tight cover to the pot so that no steam can escape while we continue to add heat, both the pressure and temperature inside the vessel will rise. If a pressure cooker's pressure relief valve fails to release the built-up pressure within the cooker, an explosion will happen, causing serious damage. So it becomes important in cooking, and in life, that we understand how to manage the pressure that builds up on the inside. Without a release valve, life's pressures will lead to dangerous explosions. Here are three ways to help release life's pressure: 1) speak with integrity, 2) live with godliness, and 3) walk in humility.

THE CLIFFS OF LIFE

The cliffs of life are the most difficult to navigate because there's nowhere to go except down. Whether we jump or are pushed off by unexpected tragedy, the descent spirals quickly down to an end. We all have a parachute with a rip cord that is the only thing we can hold on to. The fiber of the rip cord is *hope*. Hope is the only thing we can grip in a death fall. Hold on to the cord and use your weight to open your parachute. Scriptures teach us that the things we see will fade away, while the things we can't see will last forever. *H*ope *O*pens *P*eople's *E*yes and allows us to see and hold on to something during the descent. Faith, or Fear Ain't In This House, gives us the ability to pull the cord. Love, Living Outside of a Vulnerable Experience, is the intangible air we can walk on in our fall. The writer Paul describes hope, faith, and love and says the greatest is love. Hold on! You are loved!

CHANGE YOUR HABITS—PART ONE: DON'T BE A ROCKING HORSE

Life is racing by, and we are an extremely busy society. We are burning up hours, days, months, and years without purpose while the cemeteries are being filled with unused potential. A rocking horse keeps moving but doesn't go anywhere while carving a rut. Today, we focus on changing the habits in our lives that have carved ruts, and tomorrow we will focus on letting go of the old habits and catapulting into God's purpose and plan for our lives. Paul sums up the struggle we all face regarding life's bad habits that trip us: "I want to do what is right, I inevitably do what is wrong" (Rom. 7:21). The Bible gives us rut-buster habits. If we can change our old habits and apply these new ones, we will find purpose and direction for our lives. Get off your rocking horse by making new habits:

- Habit of time with God's Word
- Habit of prayer
- Habit of giving
- Habit of serving others

CHANGE YOUR HABITS—PART TWO: POLE-VAULTING INTO GOD'S PLAN

Yesterday, we set the bar with four rut-buster habits that will get us off the rocking horse and catapult us into God's plan (reading scriptures, praying, giving, and serving). Today, we focus on a life plan to activate those habits that will pole-vault us into a new, powerful life filled with purpose and direction. A pole-vaulter must do four things to get over the bar:

1) Get into a mind-set. "Set your minds on things that are above, not on things that are on earth" (Col. 3:2).
2) Strain forward. "So take a new grip with your tired hands, stand firm on your shaky legs, and mark out a straight, smooth path for your feet" (Heb. 12:12).
3) Sprint ahead. "Forget what is behind, run toward the goal" (1 Corin. 9:12).
4) Finish strong. "Well done, good and faithful servant!" (Matt. 25:1).

The other side of the bar is the victory we all have in Christ. So grab your pole, set your mind, strain forward, sprint ahead, and finish strong as you jump ahead.

THE ANTIDOTE FOR COMPLAINING

Complaining is like a virus. It gets into our systems and goes through us like a disease. It takes the joy out of our spirits, turns peace into chaos, turns positivity into negativity, turns success into failure, and changes good relationships to bad ones. The best antidote for complaining is to be grateful. A grateful attitude changes perception and reality.

- **G**rateful: Being grateful and negative is like mixing oil and water. It is impossible to be grateful and negative at the same time.
- **R**elease: When we complain, we hold on to and squeeze whatever it is that is bothering us. Releasing loosens the grip of complaining and allows us to be open to collecting new information.
- **A**lign: Being grateful realigns us with positive things.
- **T**hink: Being grateful allows us to think about things that are positive and good.
- **E**ncourage: Instead of complaining about what people have done wrong, focus on what they have done right.
- **F**light: Being grateful allows us to run away from the things that grip us.
- **U**nderstanding: Being grateful brings an awareness and understanding to things we would otherwise complain about.
- **L**earn: Being grateful gives us the ability to learn from the good and the bad.

YOU CAN CHANGE IN CONFLICT

People react and respond differently to situations of conflict. The following guide will help us understand these behaviors. (Reese, Brandt, & Howie, *Effective Human Relations*).

Behaviors Exhibited by Nonassertive, Assertive, and Aggressive people			
	Nonassertive Person	**Assertive Person**	**Aggressive Person**
In conflict situations	Avoids conflict	Communicates directly	Dominates
In decision-making situations	Allows others to choose	Chooses for self	Chooses for self and others
In situations expressing feelings	Holds true feelings inside	Open, direct, and honest while allowing others to express their feelings	Expresses feelings in a threatening manner; puts down and inhibits others
In group meeting situations	Uses indirect, unclear statements: "Would you mind if ...?"	Uses direct, clear "I" statements: "I believe that ..."	Uses clear, demeaning "you" statements: "You should know better!"

Ideally, the middle ground, Assertive Person, is one to strive for. There are many resources to help you in your quest to manage conflict in a positive way. Take the steps necessary for you to change your behavior, and you will be surprised at the impact on the behavior of and change in others. You can change in conflict.

WHEN CHANGE IS IN THE AIR—PART ONE

What should we do when change is inevitable? Sometimes we see it coming, and other times we get blindsided. Change is never easy. People in general find it very difficult to embrace something new. We are creatures of habit, and the older we get the more settled we get in our own ways. In many cases, when people are faced with a change, they will choose to do nothing rather than do something. There are many consequences that result from not adapting to change. Businesses fail, relationships end, and opportunities are lost if we are not open to change. Let's look at a few tools to use when we are faced with a fork in the road. First, *choose happiness*. What we choose to focus on largely determines our level of happiness. Our thoughts control our actions, which determine our results. Instead of seeing change as the end of something, see it as the beginning of something new. If we can mentally reframe things that make us unhappy into something that makes us happy, we can learn to skip rather than fall.

WHEN CHANGE IS IN THE AIR—PART TWO

The second key to accepting change is to *stay positive*. Positive thoughts pave the road for positive attitudes and effective relationships. One of the first casualties of change that we view as negative is our relationships. Staying positive adds mortar between the bricks. We have a choice to swim in one of two pools, the positive or the negative. Either pool will soak you. Third, *keep an open mind*. Too often, we try to manage a direction in which we think things are going and forget that God is in control. If I can expose myself to information and experiences beyond what I know, I will mature and become more complete. One of the most powerful tools we can ever use in life is flexibility. It opens doors that appear to be locked tight. In the words of Jesus, "Let not your hearts be troubled. Believe in God; believe also in me" (John 14:1).

Understanding the importance of change is critical in certain situations. Choosing to accept change can establish positive outcomes in our lives and in the lives of others. These three tools—choosing happiness, staying positive, and keeping an open mind—will help you when change is in the air.

WHAT'S IN YOUR TANK?

My first experience of a small Midwest town parade was "sweet." Personal lawnmowers, tractors, and wagons traveled down a designated road as their drivers threw out candy. Picture your life as an automobile, and as you navigate your way through the roads of life, you have an opportunity to distribute sweet gifts. After you encounter several potholes and barriers, your vehicle breaks down. You trade in your earthly vehicle for a heavenly one (salvation). The new car needs fuel to get off the lot (Holy Spirit). If you keep your car Spirit fueled and filled, you will see nine fruits fill the inside of your vehicle: love, joy, peace, forbearance, kindness, goodness, faithfulness, gentleness, and self-control. As we stay on our heavenly road, we are given gifts to distribute that will benefit others. The scriptures are full of the gifts of the Holy Spirit. If you want a vehicle that is heaven bound, full of the fruits of the Holy Spirit and gifts that will benefit others, it is time to trade the old one in for a new one and fuel it with heavenly power.

DRAMA DRAINS

Have you ever been around someone for whom their entire life revolves around drama? Whether you know someone or you are that someone, I have breaking headline news for you DRAMA DRAINS!!!!!!! Drama is like the quicksand that sucks you and from which you can't get out. Common ground for drama is idle time. It always seems that when there is a lull or quiet time or place, someone feels the need to fill the void with drama. There are drama queens, blamers, know-it-alls, whiners, backstabbers, complainers, naysayers, gossipers, and aggressors who all contribute to drama. Now that I have identified myself and those of you who are reading this, step back and don't get caught up in the hamster wheel of drama that never ends. Many times, we are not aware that we are contributing and/or participating in something that has a negative overtone. If the things we say or do don't benefit someone or something it is best to stay away and avoid contact and meddling. Drama is a huge recruiter of those who would listen and join. If you bring drama to the table, there is a good chance you'll be eating alone. Just sayin!!

CHOOSING YOUR BATTLEGROUND VERSUS CHOOSING YOUR BATTLES

My pastor and dear friend stirred a thought that might help us understand our daily struggles and put them into a new perspective. We have all heard and applied the phrase "choose your battles." I am going to challenge that thinking because one thing's for certain— we will never run out of battles. There are two battlegrounds with two end results. One is kingdom-based, one is earth-based. One has a good ending, and the other—not so much. The battles are the same, but we get to choose the battleground. Let's talk about relational dysfunction. The events and circumstances are the same, but where we fight is the difference. Kingdom battlegrounds are motivated by hope, joy, patience, forgiveness, and victory, while earthly battlegrounds are motivated by pain, anger, desperation, fear, and unforgiveness. Kingdom battlegrounds have a future, while earthly battlegrounds have a dead end. So the question to ask yourself is, "What is at the end of my battles? Am I fighting for kingdom principles, or am I fighting and going nowhere?" Each battlefield will give you its own pair of glasses, its own set of eyes. I don't know about you, but I prefer kingdom eyes.

WHERE YOU GONNA LIVE?—PART ONE

With all the events and circumstances in life, one thing is for certain. We are either in a storm, going into a storm, or coming out of a storm. No matter what season we are in, we have to deal with problems and opportunities every day of our lives. We are created physically, emotionally, and spiritually. Let's examine the spiritual side of our being and explore three different choices to build and take up residence in. Where we choose to live spiritually determines the outcome of our lives. I recently visited Kansas City's football (Arrowhead) and baseball (Kauffman) stadiums. They have a huge parking lot that services both arenas. This facility provides a great representation of the three residential places that are described in scripture. One arena is the Old Testament, and the second is the New Testament. The parking lot represents the world outside the arenas. The Old Testament is anchored in the law that was given through Moses. The New Testament is founded and built on grace and truth through the death, life, and resurrection of Jesus. The world represents everyone outside of the New Testament and the Old Testament.

WHERE YOU GONNA LIVE?—PART TWO

Picture the cross from the bottom to the top. Arms extend outward on both sides. The cross represents a connecting point for all three arenas. With Arrowhead, Kauffman, and a huge parking lot surrounding them, imagine the foot of the cross inside the OT arena and the head of the cross inside the NT arena. The sides of the cross extend into either side of the parking lot. The only entrance into the NT arena is through the cross from the foot (OT arena) and the sides (parking lot). We have one of three choices of where to live: 1) in the legalism of the law, 2) in the darkness of the parking lot, or 3) in the light of Jesus. The brilliance of the stadium lights of all who are in Christ are welcoming you to walk from darkness (the parking lot) and legalism of religion (the Old Testament) into eternal grace and truth (the New Testament). The walk from the Old Testament arena and from the parking lot is led by the path of the cross to the New Testament. The arms of the cross and the base of the cross are extending a welcoming path to eternal grace and truth in the New Testament arena. The choice is yours. Where you gonna live?

WHERE IS GOD?

Have you ever asked where God is at some point in your life? Maybe you have experienced a traumatic life loss in unfortunate circumstances. Maybe it was property loss from an accident or catastrophic disaster or perhaps an inability to sell a home or get a job. There are events and circumstances that surround us daily from a personal, local, statewide, national, and worldwide influence. These could have a negative impact on us that causes us to question the existence of God. My pastor shared something very insightful: "God doesn't show up in our lives to keep bad things from happening to us…. God shows up in our lives so that even when bad things happen, we will continue to trust Him." I have spent a lifetime responding to and helping people in crisis. I can assure you that none of us will escape the misfortunes of this life as we know it. The one thing we do have is a God who provides comfort and peace in the midst of the storms we face. We cannot escape the trials and tribulations of life, but we can have hope for what the future will bring. Knowing God is our escape into the future.

MANAGING THE HEAT

I was subject to extreme amounts of heat while growing up in the deserts of Nevada. I remember frying eggs on the sidewalk, carrying extra towels to wrap around the steering wheel and placing them on the car seats to prevent burning, and having my feet sink while walking as the extreme heat melted the asphalt. in our local area, state, country, and world, the heat is on. The disasters, a divided nation of people, terrorism, and threat of nuclear war have amped the heat up on a global level. Be encouraged in the middle of the heat wave that there is a cooling and peaceful presence. No matter how hot it gets there is a cool towel to wrap around our thoughts, our hearts, and our hands to keep us from melting under the circumstances. "The Lord is near. Do not be anxious about anything, but in every situation, by prayer and petition, with thanksgiving, present your requests to God. And the peace of God, which transcends all understanding, will guard your hearts and your minds in Christ Jesus." I learned physical survival in the desert with resources and preparedness. I am continuing to learn survival in the spiritual world with God's resources and God's preparedness. The Heat Is On!

HEAVEN RESULTS IN THE WORST CIRCUMSTANCES

Have you ever had an event, circumstance, or situation knock the wind out of you only to find that it turned out to be part of God's plan for you? When we are inconvenienced or displaced, it is normal to focus on those things. We become anxious, frustrated, angry, and emotional. Jesus and His family experienced all of these things and more. Yet He survived to become one of the most celebrated figures in the history of mankind. "'For I know the plans I have for you,' declares the LORD, 'plans to prosper you and not to harm you, plans to give you hope and a future'" (Jer. 29:11). A source of comfort is knowing that God is in charge no matter how tough it looks from our side of heaven. "As the heavens are higher than the earth, so are my ways higher than your ways and my thoughts than your thoughts" (Isa. 55:9). There are two ripples that result from "stuff"—an earthly ripple and a heavenly ripple. The ripple effect felt by those around us is determined by what we soak in. I want heavenly ripples!

OVERSENSITIVITY

If you are like me, it is easy to take some things personally. We have lots of unmet expectations that could lead to internal conflict. One of my personal battles is the need to be accepted. When I feel like I am not, I have anxieties that lead to self-doubt. My perception is blurred because of my insecurities. One of the things I have corrected in my journey of being oversensitive is to be polite and courteous without expecting anything in return. Another example of oversensitivity is not being able to take criticism. If we can look at criticism as a tool to grow and learn, it becomes constructive and not destructive. Have you ever been cut off in traffic and lost it? Road rage is usually a result of unresolved conflict within a person. The traffic event triggers unrest within us that hasn't been recognized or dealt with. If we can all step back, take a breath, and observe the situation, we can learn to control our reactions. We don't have to take things personally. We can choose to not become upset. Replace negative thinking with positive thinking. If we can let things go, the power of oversensitivity goes with it.

THE POWER
OF FOUR WORDS

I was recently asked to visit an elderly woman who was suffering from severe depression. She had lost her husband fifteen years prior, a son two years prior, and a grandson two months prior. I was the celebrant for her grandson's funeral, where I met her for the first time. One of the hardest things our elderly people face is outliving the ones they lived for. There feel there is no hope and no reason to live. This loving woman was curled up in bed wanting to die. As soon as I consoled her, she broke into a flood of tears. She had no desire to continue in anything; she had stopped eating and getting out of bed. After listening and crying with her, the conversation shifted to giving her something to look for beyond the grave. We began to talk about looking and focusing toward a glimpse of heaven. Her countenance changed as she began to anticipate something beyond the pain and loss she was soaking in. I gave her a prescription to repeat four words over and over. As I helped her with these words, she began reciting on her own. I told her she had to repeat these four words one hundred to five hundred times a day. They were, "I love you, God!"

September 11

A DAY OF MOURNING

I was teaching a 6:00 a.m. spin class in Las Vegas, Nevada. The entire fitness center came to a stilled quiet, and we all hovered around TV sets to gather information on the horrific events that were spreading across every news outlet. On September 11, 2001, at 8:45 a.m. (EDT), a beautiful Tuesday morning, a hijacked American Airlines Boeing 767 loaded with twenty thousand gallons of jet fuel crashed into the North Tower of the World Trade Center in New York City. Two other planes, within the hour, crashed into the South Tower and the Pentagon. A fourth hijacked plane crashed in a rural field in western Pennsylvania. Close to three thousand people died in this horrific attack, including a staggering 415 first responders. The entire world was shocked and stunned as the events hit the media. As we honor the fallen from this historic loss in US history, may we all feel a sense of patriotism to our country and what it stands for. Let us put the brakes on and have a moment of silence as we remember this day.

September 12

WHY TO HOW IN GRIEF

In the grieving process, one of the most difficult questions we face is "Why?" When someone we love is facing imminent death or passes, our whole world flips, causing confusion, anxiety, and chaos. The *why* questions can be never ending, causing us to lose sleep and the ability to function. There are seldom satisfying answers in our search for meaning. Changing the *why* to *how* over time can help provide some comfort in the effort to reassemble pieces from a shattered world that doesn't make any sense. When you are ready, make the *how* questions just as persistent as the *why* questions. Here are a few questions you can ask:

- How can I carry the torch in honor and memory of my loved one?
- How would my loved one want me to live?
- How can I use the things my loved one taught me to teach others?
- How can I learn positive coping skills?
- How can I open myself up to relationships in a new way?
- How can I help others in their grieving process?
- How can I keep the memories alive?

I have personally changed my mind-set from *why* to *how* in coping with death. This has helped me in my life mission of helping people get to a better place. God's peace in your journey.

WHEN GOD SHOWS UP

There is nothing more satisfying in life than to get out of the way and watch God show up. I was officiating a veteran's graveside funeral when I experienced the most powerful witness to God's presence and glory. After the twenty-one-gun salute and playing of taps, I began to close in prayer. A gust of wind came and lifted the flag off the casket, where it hovered perfectly for forty-five to sixty seconds. My reaction was to stay still and say nothing. After the flag lowered flawlessly back onto the casket, there was complete silence, which lasted about ten minutes as everyone present was in awe at being in the presence of Almighty God. When I broke the silence, I was breathless and could barely utter a word. But we still had to continue in the moment as the flag was folded and presented to the honored widow. This was over twenty-five years ago, and the influence that event had on my life was and still is profound. Sometimes we just have to get out of the way when God shows up.

ATTITUDE FOR LIVING

I am always looking for mentors to teach me how to live with everything within me to its fullest potential. One of my life heroes is Leroy Robert "Satchel" Paige. Paige grew up in difficult times and had to fight through adversity as a baseball player in the Negro Southern League. He was the first pitcher from the Negro leagues to play in the 1948 World Series. His outstanding achievements as an African American athlete paved his way into the National Baseball Hall of Fame in 1971. His infectious, enthusiastic, cocky, and warm personality made him much bigger than any baseball award. "Work like you don't need the money. Love like you've never been hurt. Dance like nobody's watching." This quote not only got my attention; it became an attitude to adopt in my personal life. Thank you, Satchel, for not giving in to the challenges and voices that could have taken the wind out of your sails. Here is what I can learn; 1) Work with passion and heart, 2) love outside of pain, and 3) don't be concerned about what others think and say.

CHARACTER VERSUS KINGDOM

My son schooled me on some thinking that I totally believe in when he returned from a retreat that focused on training young men to build their character rather than their kingdom. The "kingdom" thought is focused on building your life around your career, your properties, and your future investments. It is about setting your future with wise planning and doing everything you can to achieve your goals. The "character" thought is to establish your identity on who you are rather than what you have or what you have obtained. I have always defined *character* and *integrity* as the alignment of your head, your heart, and your hands. When what I think, feel, and do are all on the same page, I am truly moving in a productive and maturing direction. If what I obtain (my kingdom) is in conflict with my core being (character), then life becomes a journey at the expense of others. If who I am is in alignment with my heart, mind, and hands, then life becomes a journey of benefitting others. It is possible for two people to have the same goals but different paths. This is *great* advice. Thank you, son!

WHEN LIFE
THROWS YOU A CURVEBALL

One of my favorite memories as a kid was playing catch with my dad in the backyard. He was grooming me to play the position of catcher. One time he threw me a curveball that missed my glove and hit me square in the face. I had both eyes blackened and my lips were doubled in size with a bright purple tint. I wasn't expecting that pitch and didn't see it coming. Too often in life we are thrown curveballs that can take spiritual, emotional, and physical tolls on us. They are pitches that come out of nowhere. It could be the dreaded early a.m. phone call with devastating news, it could be the results from medical tests or MRIs, it could be the loss of family, friend, or pet, or it could be the loss of income. The curveballs are endless and devastating. The best thing I have learned in life is to believe and trust in something beyond the event or circumstance. Seeing, believing, and trusting in something brings hope. Right behind hope comes encouragement. And right behind encouragement comes perseverance. We have to see beyond, believe beyond, walk beyond, and live beyond the curveballs of life

COMPASSION FATIGUE

Are you a deeply caring individual? Do you identify with the needs of others before your own? Are your antennas always tuned in to helping people or animals who are suffering or have been traumatized by an unfortunate event? People like us are known as caregivers. Some of us have been taught at an early age to care for others' needs before our own. Others have been forced into a caring atmosphere as a loved one became dependent on us. Whether it is a choice of full-time or part-time work or baptism by fire, caregivers are subject to a high level of compassion fatigue. Day in and day out, we struggle to function because we are constantly in the presence of heart-wrenching physical demands along with emotional challenges. This painful reality along with society's blatant disregard for those who are fragile and frail puts a whole lot of stress on caregivers. If we are not aware of the blindsiding effects of chronic stress, we can become overwhelmed, insensitive, and sidetracked. Eventually, negative attitudes can prevail. Accepting the presence of compassion fatigue in your life only serves to validate the fact that you are a deeply caring individual. Ongoing self-care will fill your tank. Authentic and sustainable self-care begins with you: enhance your awareness with education, clarify your personal boundaries, be kind to yourself, talk and listen to other caregivers, eat healthfully, develop consistent sleep patterns, and take a "rest area" exit off the interstate of care.

WORKING PARENTS

Are you a working parent who goes home every night to a pile of laundry, uncut grass, and household chores calling your name? Are the weekends filled with stress from trying to play catch-up? Are you guilt ridden because the kids take on the role of a liability instead of an asset to your life? Here are some tools that can help working parents and kids reconnect:

- Talk to your kids. You will be surprised at how much they understand.
- Involve yourself with a common interest that you both can enjoy.
- Minutes are very important. Carve out thirty minutes to play catch, read a book, or watch a show.
- Escape from the demands of the day and use this time as an oasis with your family.

We must look at our kids as gifts and unwrap them every day in the chaos and hustle of life's demands.

COMMUNICATION IS A FULL MEAL

The first words we speak can set the table for a good or bad meal of communication. "Pleasing words are like honey. They are sweet to the soul and healing to the bones" (Prov. 16:24). The last words we leave on the plate can have a lingering effect as they sink into the mind of the hearer. "Let your words be few" (Ecc. 5:2). Once we realize the tremendous impact we can have in the beginning and the end of an interaction, we can help control the outcome of the communication process. Here are a few utensils we can use to help serve the best meal:

- Begin each conversation with a compliment. If we can start off with an honest and positive reflection of something or someone that is relevant to the conversation, we have served the first course as a wonderful appetizer.
- When the conversation is coming to a close, offer genuine appreciation for the interaction. This will leave a good taste with the parties involved.
- We have all experienced a form of food poisoning at some time in our life and the uncomfortable aftereffects. Bad communication can have the same effects as we wrestle with the sharp pains and cramps.

Let's be as proactive as we can in our daily interactions. Be complimentary and grateful for every meal.

WORDS CAN OPEN OUR EARS

Sometimes a few words can encourage you and shift your thoughts to a positive direction. Here are a few thoughts that I hope will help you on your journey:

- The best part of family is knowing that you are part of it.
- Growing is mature. Giving is maturing.
- A surrendered life is a changed life.
- Our earthly identity is passed on to us, and our heavenly identity is given to us.
- An excuse is an escape from responsibility.
- Forbidden fruit creates many jams.
- If you don't want to reap the fruits of sin, stay out of the devil's orchard.
- Don't give up. Moses was once a basket case.
- Every core is surrounded with seeds.
- The greatest reward from a relationship is not what you get out of it but what you become through it.

THE LEAVES ARE CHANGING

Fall is an incredible season. I was on the East Coast one year and was inspired to write a song while walking in a group of trees and picking up handfuls of brilliant leaves that had fallen on the ground.

The leaves are changing and so am I.
There are so many colors, the ones I have inside.
Some leaves are on fire. Some are rusted brown.
Some leaves are withered, and some are profound.
Open my heart Lord, and teach me to be
Like the leaves on the ground, falling free.
Some trees are bare now.
They've bared their souls.
They're starting over. They've just let go
Just as a baby whose life has begun.
Molding in the image of God's saving son
Open my heart Lord, and teach me to be
Like the leaves on the ground, falling free.

OVERCOMING THE PAST

It's impossible to succeed in life without overcoming the past. We spend far too much time and energy on things we can't change rather than on the most important thing we can change—our attitudes. Life is like an automobile that can spin off the road. We must get out of the ditch and keep moving forward. Here are some important things to do to get back on the road:

- Get back in the driver's seat.
- Keep looking through the front windshield.
- Use the rearview mirror to remind you where you came from.
- Know where you came from because it is paving the way for where you are going.
- Most important: keep your foot on the gas or you won't go anywhere.

OUR WORDS HAVE A RIPPLE EFFECT

As a rock creates a ripple when it is dropped into a puddle of water, our words also create a ripple when they are dropped on ears. Our words go well beyond the initial impact. It is very wise to choose our words well because we have no idea who they are going to affect. Here are some things to think about before we speak:

- Words can build or destroy.
- Words can encourage or discourage.
- Words can heal or hurt.
- Words can motivate or deflate.

Many times our careless words are meaningless chatter when we have nothing to contribute. Let's be swift to hear and slow to speak.

CONFLICT RESOLUTION: "PIZZA STYLE"

I love pizza, especially when each slice has its own savory flavor. In a recent study of Proverbs 19:11–12, I took a bite of twelve of the best pieces of conflict resolution "pizza style." I invite you take this combo supreme out of the oven and enjoy the ingredients that will help us all become better communicators in our struggles with conflict.

1) Walk away.
2) Spread dew (a result of cooling in hot air).
3) Don't be foolish, and don't look for an argument.
4) Seek understanding.
5) Be alert and sober minded.
6) Be disciplined in the Word.
7) Give. It takes your eyes off your own circumstances.
8) Draw the line and stick to it.
9) Don't enable.
10) Get godly counsel.
11) Give your plans to God.
12) Stay loyal.

Solomon has given us great advice. It is up to us to apply it.

THE POWER
OF SANDPAPER

Sandpaper has a purpose—to smooth out roughness. The grain used depends on the surface that needs to be sanded and smoothed. *The greatest reward from a relationship is not what we get out of it but what we become through it.* If we can focus on conflict as a chance to grow rather than the pain and bleeding from the process, we can become mature and complete through it. The struggles we have in life make our surface very rough. The relationships we have not only sand our edges, but they allow us to be smooth for others to come near to. Here are a few things to think about:

- View conflict as positive sandpaper.
- The rougher it is, the more I can learn.
- Go through the process of sanding knowing that the end result will be better.

OVERCOMING PERFECTIONISM

The thinking of a perfectionist can be very harmful. Perfectionists believe it is catastrophic if they make a mistake. When situations are out of control or don't go their way, they could become quite upset. Anger and bitterness can creep in when their high expectations aren't met. Relational difficulties, emotional problems, physical setbacks, and spiritual dysfunction are signs and symptoms of being a perfectionist. Here are some tools to combat perfectionism:

- Learn and grow from your mistakes instead of beating yourself up.
- Take time to stop and enjoy the seasons of your life. Find happiness and joy in your circumstances.
- Accept yourself as being good enough to move on to the next task rather than trying to perfect every task in front of you. With the number of responsibilities and tasks we face daily, it is unreasonable to complete them all exceptionally well.
- Spending too much time on one activity to do it perfectly could delay other tasks that need to be done. Set reasonable and realistic time limits.
- Not everything is black and white. Perfectionists miss the shade of gray, which is critical for understanding different perspectives.
- Goals need to be small, tangible, achievable, and realistic.

WHY AM I LIVING?

Life's demands have a tendency to bankrupt us for our purpose on earth. Millions of people have crashed and burned, which makes our gravesites the wealthiest places on earth. Our desires are the driving force behind the wheel of life. Do my desires benefit others or me? "We are created to do good works which God prepared in advance for us to do" (Eph. 2:10). Consider the ant. The ant has two stomachs, one for its own needs and one for the colony it serves. Let's look at our desires:

- Does my work benefit the "colony" I serve?
- Are my desires in harmony with my passion?
- Am I caught in the hamster wheel, spinning out of control?

God's plan for your life is waiting for you. "Ask and it will be given to you, seek and you will find; knock and the door will be opened to you" (Matt. 7:7).

WORDS ARE POWERFUL

Do you remember when you were taught as a kid the famous comeback, "Sticks and stones may break my bones, but words will never hurt me"? *Wrong.* "Handle them carefully, for words have more power than atom bombs" (Pearl Strachan). I'm sure you have been the recipient of words of wisdom, words of encouragement, and words of praise. I am also sure you've been the recipient of condescending words, words that hurt, words that destroyed your spirit, or words that made you angry. Here are three ways we can choose to use words to benefit us and others:

- **Words received:** Words can help us. "Fools think their own way is right, but the wise listen to others" (Prov. 3:15).
- **Words spoken:** Words can have a positive influence. "Let everything you say be good and helpful, so that your words will be an encouragement to those who hear them" (Eph. 4:29).
- **Words unspoken:** Be quiet. "Keep your mouth shut and you will stay out of trouble" (Prov. 21:23).

OVERCOMING BITTERNESS—PART ONE

When bitterness takes root in a person's life, it can be a poison to relationships, to organizations, and to churches. Once planted, it will grow quickly and cause trouble. Actions will be done and words will be said that cannot be taken back. Here are some tools to guide those who are heading in the wrong direction:

- **Forgive:** We must not pretend that everything is okay. Forgiveness is the act of surrendering our desire to retaliate or get revenge. Forgiveness is the antibiotic we can put on a wound that allows healing to take place.
- **Stop talking:** Telling the story of what happened to you again and again in a negative way to everyone you meet is often a form of keeping yourself stuck in the mud. It might be harder than we think to not mention what happened to us at all for some time, but give it a try. We don't need to build allies.
- **Take responsibility:** Take what responsibility you can. If you see that you are part of the bitterness, accept that and move forward. Many people who are bitter are too ashamed to admit to it.

OVERCOMING BITTERNESS—PART TWO

Overcoming bitterness will allow us to get back a part of our lives that we have lost. These tools can hopefully help us reestablish values and comfort our damaged souls.

- **Stop building your case:** We have a need to build an army in our pain and bitterness. It becomes a war within us, and the bigger our army is, the better prepared we are for battle. The need to recruit warriors in the heat of battle is the beginning of an outside war that doesn't have a winning outcome.
- **Stop collecting evidence:** The need for validating our bitterness is addictive. We will go out of our way to spy. It's like we become private detectives. Our thoughts, time, and actions are consumed with finding new information.
- **Focus on the future:** Too often we lose sight of anything positive when we are steeped in our bitterness. Scraping the mud off the windshield gives us something to hope for. Hope puts our eyes on something beyond our stuff.
- **Professional help:** If the bitterness won't let go even after you've tried the few things mentioned, it's time to seek professional help. Working with a professional can help you see possibilities that your pain has blinded you to and give you new tools to heal the wounds that are holding you back.

THE POWER OF ONE DEGREE

The power and influence of one degree can make the difference in the total outcome of a situation, an event, or a circumstance. At 211 degrees, water is hot. At 212 degrees, water boils. The boiling water creates steam, and steam can power a locomotive. A morning cup of espresso also illustrates the power of steam. An espresso machine takes heated, pressurized water and releases it in a controlled way through coffee grounds to create that thick Italian drink. The use of steam vapor for cleaning works much the same way. Steam effectively cleans surfaces and kills viruses, bacteria, and fungi. These are just a few examples of the power of one extra degree. Let's apply this metaphor into our physical, emotional, and spiritual beings. One choice or one small shift in an attitude can change the total outcome in the results of our day, month, year, and life. Lou Holtz advised, "Want to be happy for an hour? Eat a steak. Want to be happy for a day? Play golf. Want to be happy for a week? Go on a cruise. Want to be happy for a month? Buy a new car. Want to be happy for a year? Win the lottery. Want to be happy for a lifetime? Win a championship." Adding one degree to hot water can turn something that could be negative into something more powerful than we could ever imagine. Use your one degree and win a championship in your life.

WORD UP

Have you ever spoken a word or had someone speak a word to you that came alive? There is an incredible feeling and sense of triumph when this happens. One of the greatest accounts of the Word coming to life is recorded in scripture. "In the beginning was the Word, and the Word was with God, and the Word was God" (John 1:1). "The Word became flesh and made his dwelling among us" (John 1:14). Trying to conceive of or understand this is very difficult without experiencing it. The Word truly comes alive when we believe and apply it. This next scripture has truly helped me apply and understand the power of the Word.

> So commit yourselves wholeheartedly to these words of mine. Tie them to your hands and wear them on your forehead as reminders. Teach them to your children when you're sitting in your home, and when you are on the road, and when you go to bed, and when you are getting up. Write them on the doorposts of your house and on your gates. So that your days and the days of your children may be multiplied in the land the Lord has given you. (Deut. 11:18–21)

This is a great way to lead your life. Word up!

DO IT RIGHT
THE FIRST TIME

We live in a hectic pace world that is not going to slow down. Things that were created and designed to make things simple have added confusion and chaos to our stride. Because time is quenched and our plates are full with so many things to do in the day, we sometimes look for an easy way out of doing the right thing. We cut corners or don't give the needed effort to have successful results. I have learned the hard way that if I don't have time to do things the right way I may never have the time to do it over. Students learn in the classroom that if you don't prepare for the final exam, you will not get another chance to make up the grade. Adults in the big world learn that windows of opportunities close quickly. The difficulty we all face is to put on the brakes and do things right the first time. With all the distractions in our day, it becomes difficult to see things in the dense fog as we make decisions. Slow down and do it right the first time because you may never have another chance.

THE POWER OF NONVERBAL COMMUNICATION

Studies have shown that the communication process has been broken down to 7 percent spoken word, 38 percent voice tone and intonation, and 55 percent nonverbal. This means that *93 percent* of communication is separate from the spoken word and that all the texts and emails we send have a 93 percent chance of being misunderstood. Here is another amazing stat for you: 85 percent of conflict is a result of a misunderstanding. No wonder our personal and corporate communication is a mess. It seems like the virtual wave of communication is now done through texting. My son even asked a girl to be his girlfriend via text and broke up with her a week later the same way.

When we interact with others, we continuously give and receive wordless signals. All of our nonverbal behaviors—the gestures we make, the way we sit, our posture, our space, how fast or how loud we talk, how close we stand, how much eye contact we make, our facial expressions, our touch, our intensity, our timing—send strong messages. These messages don't stop when you stop speaking either. Even when you're silent, you're still communicating nonverbally. The ability to understand and use nonverbal communication, or body language, is a powerful tool that can help you connect with others, express what you really mean, and build better relationships.

IDEA

I recently read about an acronym from John Maxwell that exemplifies how Jesus mentored and reproduced Himself in helping His disciples live to their fullest potential. My greatest satisfaction in life is knowing that I am being used to help others get to a better place. The example of Christ is fuel for those who want to make a difference. Here is what Jesus did for His team in person and what He still does for us today.

- **Instruction:** He verbally taught. He constantly used daily routines to instruct them.
- **Demonstration:** He modeled the truth and let His men observe His life. He provided show-and-tell opportunities.
- **Experience:** He let the disciples participate and apply the truths themselves. They got to practice.
- **Assessment:** He debriefed their shared experience. He assessed their growth and gave them direction.

What a great IDEA! No matter what hat you wear, you will influence someone. Help make a difference.

THE SLOW COOKER OF LIFE

There are two slow cookers of life in which we cook our thoughts—the good one and the bad one. At the end of the day, we have one of two meals that have been cooking and simmering all day. If we can learn to hold all of our thoughts obedient to scripture (the good one), we are held captive to the freedom of God. If we let our thoughts be governed and controlled by evil (the bad one), we are held captive to those ways. We control the lid and what goes into our slow cookers. Here are some godly ingredients to put into our meals. These ingredients are recorded in 1 Peter 4:7–11. Throw them in, stir them up, and let them cook all day. This is the kind of meal I want to serve.

Slow Cooker Ingredients to Living Right

- Be alert
- Be sober-minded
- Be in prayer
- Love one another deeply
- Be hospitable
- Don't grumble
- Use your gifts
- Serve one another
- Speak the very words of God
- Serve in the strength of God
- In all things, give praise through Jesus

YOU THINK
YOU HAD A BAD DAY?

Have you ever had one of those days that you thought was going to get better after something really good happened? You get surprised and excited only to find out that what happened wasn't what you thought it was going to be. Forty-one verses in John 9 are about a no-name man who was blind at birth and had settled into his lonely existence by begging for money on the street corner. He had been judged, labeled, and sentenced to a life of isolation and poverty because of his disability. Out of nowhere, some guy puts mud on his eyes and tells him to wash. His eyes were opened for the first time. But what should have been a party and celebration turned into a nightmare. His friends freaked out and turned him over to the authorities, who interrogated him and assaulted his character and integrity. His parents, who were called in for validation, abandoned him and betrayed him. He was put on trial, thrown out, and sentenced to the streets again all because he had experienced a miracle—only this time it was worse because he could see everything. His short-lived fire of new life was snuffed out by the wet blanket of his past. In his darkest moment, Jesus showed up and gave him a new identity as he believed and worshipped. Those two acts, belief and worship, will keep us off the streets of life as we learn to navigate the streets of heaven.

THE POWER OF FAITH

When the Trans-Alaskan Pipeline was being built, many Texans went to Alaska to work. The Texans could work only a few hours in the frigid weather, yet the Eskimos could work indefinitely in the cold. A physiological study showed no difference in skin thickness, blood, or any other physical feature that would explain the difference in the ability to withstand the temperatures. The solution was revealed when researchers conducted a psychological study. The difference was that the Eskimos focused on the job that had to be done, while the Texans focused on the weather.

You and I will focus daily on one of two things. We will either focus on how bad things are (the trials and temptations), or we will focus on the good that's around the corner. Jesus made it from the garden to Calvary because He focused on the job that had to be done. Godly faith can help us face and overcome every obstacle when we jump the hurdle believing in the good that is on the other side.

YOU ARE NOT ALONE

Have you ever been so overwhelmed and thought, "My odds don't look good"? I am being schooled by an incredible woman who is facing multiple diseases, the most horrific death sentence that I have ever witnessed. She is Jesus with skin as her strength to love and release her husband and others in their suffering for her is a witness of God's love. All through scripture, God's love multiplies Himself for us to fight as He gives us victory through the cross.

> For I am convinced that nothing can ever separate us from his love. Death can't, and life can't. The angels won't, and all the powers of hell itself cannot keep God's love away. Our fears for today, our worries about tomorrow, or where we are—high above the sky, or in the deepest ocean—nothing will ever be able to separate us from the love of God demonstrated by our Lord Jesus Christ when he died for us. (Rom. 8:38–39)

I want to thank my friend for teaching the power of *love* over death. You are a true witness that "You Are Not Alone."

I BECOME A PRISONER TO THE INFLUENCES IN MY LIFE

There are many influences that enslave us, both negative and positive. These influences have the power and ability to change the course of our futures. The influence of addictions and emotions can control our existence. The power of influence is too strong for us to ignore. Whether children, teenagers, or adults, we are all susceptible to influence. Paul, the apostle, acknowledged this in his letter to the church at Ephesus: "For this reason I, Paul, am prisoner of Christ Jesus for the sake of you" (Eph. 3:1). Paul realized the power of influence and chose to imprison himself to the protection and authority of the scriptures. In our society, we view prisons as facilities to protect us from those who have been influenced in a bad way. In the eyes of believers, becoming a prisoner of Christ is our protection from the influences on the outside of God's prison walls. Knowing and believing God allows us to come under a divine influence that changes the course of our future and protects us from the elements and dangers of the adversary. Our ultimate victory over the bad influences in life is to become protected by the divine presence of the Word of God.

IS THIS A SAD TIME OF YEAR?

Do you have difficulty with getting motivated and doing the things you would normally do during the winter? SAD is seasonal affective disorder with symptoms starting in the fall and carrying through the winter months. The feeling of the "winter blues" can sap your energy and cause mood changes. If you have noticed a pattern of depression for more than two years that could include disruptive sleep patterns, changes in appetite, a sense of hopelessness, thoughts of suicide, or engaging in self-destructive behaviors like drinking alcohol, doing drugs, or partaking in pornography for comfort and relaxation, then you might consider seeing your doctor. SAD is very common in areas where there is diminished sunlight and cold temperatures. The decrease in sunlight could cause a drop in serotonin (brain chemical that affects mood) along with a change in melatonin (sleep patterns and mood). One of the best physical treatments for SAD is light therapy. One of the best *soul* treatments for SAD and any depression is understanding the power of light over darkness. When we allow light into our darkest areas, we can see things that we've never seen before. "You are the light of the world. Let your light so shine before men, that they may see your good works and glorify your Father in heaven" (Matt. 5:16). When our lights shine, our darkness goes away and we can illuminate those around us.

CREATIVITY SOLVES PROBLEMS

I love the television show *MacGyver* and am so glad it has been resurrected for another series. The attraction for me is how creativity can solve problems. I make it a point to surround myself with creative people because they find a way to make things work and make things happen. Lee Iacocca said, "We are continually faced by great opportunities brilliantly disguised as insoluble problems." People who are solution-focused are always looking for opportunities to make things right. There is such positive influence and energy when solutions outweigh problems. People understand solutions much easier than problems. A mind that is constantly churning is a mind that doesn't give up. I work with two MacGyvers, and I often sit back in awe and soak up how they manage people and situations with ingenuity and resourcefulness. I have learned to be creative in raising my kids, loving my wife, and dedicating my passions in the workplace. Doing things outside of the box might not always work, but living outside the box allows for mistakes and room to explore new and creative ways to exist. We are all created to have creativity. If you want to solve more problems, get in touch with your creative side and become part of the solution, not part of the problem.

THE POWER OF A PERSONAL MISSION STATEMENT

A personal mission statement helps us find purpose, desire, and direction. Thirty-six years ago, I was assigned to write a mission statement in an international marketing class at the University of Nevada, Las Vegas. I was then challenged to shrink it down to one sentence or phrase. Little did I know that this exercise would establish a lane for me to run in for the rest of my life. George Washington Carver said, "No individual has any right to come into this world and go out of it without leaving behind him distinct and legitimate reasons for having passed through it." Here is what my mission statement, "Helping people get to a better place," has done for me: 1) it has given me a purpose for living, 2) it has given me a desire to keep going, and 3) it has given me discipline to run in the lane I was made for. My personal mission statement motivates me and allows me to live to my fullest potential, live in the present, and evaluate my progress. Here is my challenge to you: write a personal mission statement. You *will* find purpose, desire, and direction motivated by the very reason for which you were created to live. Godspeed!

YOU ARE GOOD ENOUGH

One of the many harsh things we hear in life is, "You're good but not good enough." It's like filling a balloon and then stabbing it with a needle. There was a young boy named David who was told that very thing his whole life by his dad, brothers, and others. That label sent him to the fields, where he was isolated and instructed to care for the sheep while the others did their own thing. In his loneliness, he got very good at some things and started believing in himself. During a crisis, he stepped up to the plate and took down a giant while others watched. His tool was a slingshot. In his isolation, he had practiced with all he had. You may not be the most gifted, but the lesson here is to use what you have and do your best. *You are good enough* to remove the giants that are standing in front of you. Accept yourself, get up, and keep moving forward with all you have.

HUMILITY, OPTIMISM, ENERGY

A *hoe* is a versatile agricultural tool with ancient roots. It is used to move small amounts of soil. Like the hoe, we too are used to stir up the ground around us for kingdom work. Another use of the hoe is to agitate the ground for weed removal and control, just as our role is to agitate the ground around us to remove the weeds of evil and control their existence. The hoe is also used for "hilling," which is piling soil around the base of a plant. We too are encouraged to build a foundation around the work of God as He grows and matures us and those around us. Another goal of the hoe is creating "drills," narrow furrows and shallow trenches for planting. We have opportunities every day to plant seeds for the work and glory of God. Three core values that we can implement into our being are as follows:

- **Humility:** "Do nothing out of selfish ambition or vain conceit. Rather, in humility value others above yourselves, not looking to your own interests but each of you to the interests of the others" (Phil. 4:3–4).
- **Optimism:** "We know that God makes all things work together for the good of those who love Him and are chosen to be a part of His plan" (Rom. 8:28).
- **Energy:** "Forgetting what is behind and straining toward what is ahead, I press on toward the goal to win the prize for

which God has called me heavenward in Christ Jesus" (Phil. 3:13–14).

"The difference between stumbling blocks and stepping stones is how you use them" (Unknown).

THE SHADOW KNOWS

Shadows will always provide a covering, but it is our decision to choose which shadow we sit under. There are two shadows that cover our lives. One shadow is good, and the other is bad. The good shadow will provide us with direction, purpose, and motivation to do something positive with our lives. The bad shadow will distract us, misguide us, and motivate us to do something negative. It is our choice to sit under the tree of life or the tree of death. The problem lies with the first decision. Am I being lured to do the right thing, or am I being lured to do the wrong thing? Catch yourself before you get covered by the wrong shadow. Trust your heart, instincts, and godly counsel. The shadow knows how to lead you.

CREATED
FOR RELATIONSHIPS

I remember growing up with a stinky and stagnant puddle of water in the gutter in between our house and the neighbor's house. The water was a haven for mosquitos, bugs, slime, and stench. We had to walk around it so we wouldn't be contaminated. The only thing that got rid of the cesspool was a fresh rainstorm that washed the puddle and all of its ingredients away. The same thing happens in our lives when we are isolated and separated from people. We become stagnant and smelly, and people will do everything they can to avoid us. The only remedy for healing and restoration from the bugs and stench of an isolated life is to accept and allow the flow of relationships to clean and purify us. The puddle of contaminated water that separates us and our neighbors is washed away. Please take the time to examine your curbside and see if you need to let people who care about you flow into your life.

THE TOAD LESSON

I was walking through the country on an old dirt road
When I happened to see a poor little toad
Threw down my things to lighten my load
and I placed him on my knee
He tried to jump off, but I held him tight
I tried to calm him so he'd lose his fright
I told him not to struggle or fight
'Cause he'd be safe with me
The toad, he had told me that he had no friends
He had nobody for time to spend
I told him that I'd be his friend
And together we'd be free
The outcast toad had found someone
To live in God's kingdom right under the sun
His lonely fears had been overcome
His mind was set at ease
For all you lonely people out there
You're misleading yourself and are unaware
There's always someone who is willing to share
And care for every need

WRESTLING WITH GRIEF

If you have ever been to a wrestling meet, you know how one event can have so many different weight classes with different styles, expressions, and abilities. There are several mats that are all occupied with different wrestlers. The same event has each competitor expressing a unique way of handling the pressure. Like wrestling, people respond differently to an event or circumstance that has a traumatic effect. Grieving is a very personal and highly individual experience. How one grieves depends on many factors: faith, coping mechanisms, personality, life experience, and the nature of the loss. The grieving process can't be hurried or forced. There is no normal timetable or formula. Surviving comes gradually in the shadow of time. For some it could take weeks or months. For others, it may take years. Whatever one's experience, it's critically important to be patient, to not be hard on yourself or others, and to allow this process to take its natural course.

HUMILITY BEGINS WITH UNPLUGGED EARS

Have you ever been blindsided by an irrelevant question or remark that turned a conversation or lesson in an opposite direction? A Milwaukee teacher took her first-grade class to a dairy, where a guide showed the children through the entire plant, explaining the whole process. When the tour was over, the guide asked if anyone had any questions. One little girl raised her hand. "Did you notice," she asked, "that I've got on my new snowsuit?" Whether children or adults, we have a natural tendency to make things about us. I've noticed myself thinking and waiting to talk about my stuff while listening to my wife. She could be talking about something, but I am looking for the opportunity to change the direction and focus to me. "Don't be selfish; don't try to impress others. Be humble, thinking of others as better than yourselves" (Phil. 2:3). This scripture is a challenge because it is something learned and not inherited. The nature we are born with is opposite of the nature God wants to transform us into. Humility begins with unplugged ears.

COUNT YOUR BLESSINGS

If you woke up this morning with more health than illness … you are more blessed than the million who will not survive this week.

If you have never experienced the danger of battle, the loneliness of imprisonment, the agony of torture, or the pangs of starvation … you are ahead of 500 million people in the world.

If you can attend a church meeting without fear of harassment, arrest, torture, or death … you are more blessed than three billion people in the world.

If you have food in the refrigerator, clothes on your back, a roof overhead, and a place to sleep … you are richer than 75 percent of the people in this world.

If you have money in the bank, in your wallet, under the bed, or in a dish someplace … you are among the top 8 percent of the world's wealthy.

If your parents are still alive and still married … you are very rare indeed, even in the United States and Canada.

October 22

THE TRUE CANDY OF LIFE

A man observed a sad and rugged-looking kid staring into the candy store window. He took him inside and told the cashier to fill a bag with whatever the boy wanted. The little guy's eyes got so big, and he began to fill his mouth with the incredible sugary delights. As the bag was filled and the cheeks of the young boy were bulging from the side, the man asked the lad if he could have some. The boy's joy suddenly turned into fear as he grabbed the bag, held it tight, and went running out of the store screaming, "Mine! Mine!" Sometimes in life we take for granted the heart, intention, and hand of life around us. When we hold on to things, we become selfish and ungrateful, and we miss the opportunity to receive and give. The best antidote for a selfish heart is a giving heart. True happiness doesn't come from filling our bags at the candy store. Happiness comes from helping fill others' bags with the sweet things in life. We are not supposed to be a storehouse; we're supposed to be an outlet. We are created to be a blessing to others around us. Let's look at every opportunity to fill others' bags with the true candy of life.

WOUNDED CAT

If you have ever been around a wounded cat, you know how difficult it is to offer them any help. They will find a corner and hunker down. If you reach out to offer comfort and assistance, you better be prepared for the fight of your life. They will hiss, scratch, and fend off anyone who gets close to them. Cats' defenses go into full throttle when they are injured, including pushing off any help. Sometimes, our human nature can react to injury or bad news the same way. If there is a life-threatening injury, some people might respond like a cat and find a corner. They will withdraw from family and friends and lash out at any attempt to help. Other times, a person receives bad news like cancer or other life-threatening illnesses and finds a corner to hide in. In a self-defense response, they will lash out and refuse any comfort or care from loved ones or, in some cases, professionals. The best way to handle this reaction is to offer comfort and care from a distance. In most cases, a little time will allow trust. The injured party is requiring space to assess and understand the situation. Other situations might require professional intervention. Don't be afraid to ask for counsel or guidance in responding to this most difficult situation.

HOW DOES FEAR DRIVE ME?

What do you do when you get the wind knocked out of you by a traumatic event or devastating news? Fear sets in and becomes a great motivator for one of two reactions. The end result of our reaction to fear is totally determined by the direction in which we choose to be driven. Fear (False Expectations Appearing Real) has the power to drive us down into a grave or to catapult us up and out into our faith (Fear Ain't In This House). One leads to death, and the other leads to life. Downward fear can freeze our mobility and open a huge sinkhole that pulls us down. Upward fear gives us faith, hope, and a vine with hands from heaven to pull us up and out as we hold on to the things we can't see because the things we see will fade away and the things we can't see will last forever. "The fear of the Lord is the beginning of wisdom" (Ps. 111:10). Fear can fill my backpack with heavy rocks and drive me down, or it can act as an accelerant in my tank to drive me out of Dodge. How does fear drive you?

PUBLIC PRAYER

When Lyndon Baines Johnson was president, he had several guests in for a meal at the family room of the White House. Johnson had given the honor of saying grace to journalist Bill Moyers, a former Baptist minister. As Moyers began to softly say grace, Johnson, who could not understand what was being said, interrupted Moyers and said, "Speak up, man." Without looking up and barely stopping in midsentence, Moyers replied, "I wasn't talking to you." Sometimes our prayers are meant to be heard, and sometimes they're not. If we are praying for the benefit of others in a public environment, then we need to speak up. If we are praying out loud to benefit ourselves in front of others, then we need to be silent. When asked, evaluate the circumstances and pray with honor and discretion. When not asked, keep quiet. "When you pray, don't be like those show-offs who love to stand up and pray in the meeting places and on the street corners. They do this just to look good" (Matt. 6:5). There is a fine line for public prayer.

CORRECTION IS KEY TO PERSONAL GROWTH AND SUCCESS

One of the biggest roadblocks to our personal growth and success is how we respond to correction. There is something in all of us that would rather *look* good than *be* good. Some of our responses that get in the way are interpreting correction as rejection, taking offense, becoming defensive, keeping a record, holding the person emotionally hostage, or shooting the messenger. Our egos can blindside us, and our insecurities can keep us locked up. The reality is that we need people in our lives to help us learn and grow. If we can absorb correction as a tool to become stronger and better, we are on the road to progress. Here are four qualities that are exhibited in people who are open to correction:

- **Teachability:** Open to counsel, quick to learn, and willing to listen
- **Vulnerability:** Being open to something that might hurt
- **Honesty:** Being committed to the truth no matter how much it hurts
- **Availability:** Not running or hiding but being present

If we can adopt these four characteristics, we will be on our way to being more mature and complete on our journey of life.

THE TEARS
OF A PET—PART ONE

After thirty-six years of assisting people in their grief, I have become aware of a new phenomenon concerning pets. Their tears need to be understood as they try to understand and accept the loss of their masters. I was working with a mom who had lost her twenty-three-year-old son. She asked if she could bring along his dog, who happened to be a German short-haired pointer. When we started talking about her son, the dog jumped into my lap and began lapping me, leaving my suit soaked with his love marks. I wanted to meet the mom again and asked her to bring the dog. This time, I purposefully avoided giving any contact or attention to the dog because I wanted to see what would take place. When our conversation focused on the loss of his master, the dog buried his head in my lap and began to tear up with heavy breathing. The dog had been sleeping alone in the bed of his master for eight weeks. I have seen the dog on several occasions since then, and he responds and remembers me as one who understands.

THE TEARS
OF A PET—PART TWO

When given the chance, pets will grieve with family members. So often, they are overlooked in the grieving process of life loss. One time, I was visiting with a widow in her grief of losing her lifelong husband. He had a cat that was in depression and had withdrawn for several days with no contact or presence in the house. While talking with the widow about her husband's passing, the cat came out of nowhere, jumped up onto my shoulder, and began pressing his body against the side of my neck and face. The wife said that the cat had never done that before with anyone, and she was amazed. The cat heard us talking about his master and came out of hiding in his depression. The cat purred and wept while affectionately pressing against me in the same chair that he had spent much of his life in the comfort of his master. I have now included the tears of a pet whenever possible in the grieving process. They know, hear, and understand the pain of loss. My dry-cleaning bill has doubled.

OBSERVE AND DELIVER

Here are some wise words from an anonymous poet. "If you can start the day without caffeine; if you can get going without pep pills; if you can always be cheerful, ignoring the aches and pains; if you can resist complaining and boring people with your troubles; if you can eat the same food every day and be grateful for it; if you can understand when your loved ones are too busy to give you any time; if you can forgive a friends lack of consideration; if you can overlook it when those you love take it out on you, when, through no fault of your own, something goes wrong; if you can take criticism and blame without resentment; if you can ignore a friends limited education and never correct him; if you can resist treating a rich friend better than a poor friend; if you can face the world without lies and deceit; if you can conquer tension without medical; if you can relax without liquor; if you can sleep without the aid of drugs; if you can honestly say that deep in your heart you have no prejudice against creed or color, religion or politics; then you my friend, your almost as good as your dog." This poem is dedicated to two kinds of people: 1) animal lovers, and 2) those who can **Observe and Deliver** *"Be alert, be sober minded, love each other deeply, offer hospitality, don't grumble, use whatever gift you have to serve others"* (1 Peter 4:7–10).

THE STING OF SUNBURN

Life experiences can give us sunburns of many different degrees. The third-degree burns usually result after longer exposure to the damaging rays that we allow ourselves to sit under. If I have no sunburn and someone pats me on the shoulders, I am cool with it. If I have sunburn and the same person touches me on the shoulders, I am hot with it. The person touching me is the same, but my reaction is different based on my skin condition. Anger and other emotions are skin conditions of being burnt. The most difficult understanding of our nature is that we want to blame the person or event that touched our burns. The reality is that our pain was not caused by the person or event. It was caused by our sunburn.

HOW DO RELATIONSHIPS SURVIVE A TRAUMATIC LOSS?

There is so much pain and difficulty in trying to personally cope with a traumatic loss, whether it is a death or divorce or something else. Navigating a minute, hour, week, month, or year is hard enough, let alone trying to stay connected in relationships we can't escape. I want to provide you with some tools to help you move forward in your relationships after traumatic events.

- Everyone grieves differently. Identify the differences in how you grieve.
- Acknowledge the differences, and respect others' journeys.
- Lower the expectations you have about how you believe other people should be grieving or how they should respond to your grieving.
- Find out what others' needs are. Be transparent in saying, "This is what I am struggling with, and this is how you can help me."
- Agree with one another that you will work on understanding the differences in your journey and commit to actions that are being asked of you.

The dynamics of life loss ripple through families and friends. You can be a single parent, a couple, a sibling, a family member, a friend, or all of the above. We can't escape relationships. The most trying times are in our deepest, darkest hours of loss. We must strengthen our bridges before the torrent of loss carries them away.

BEING PROACTIVE

Life can pass us by if we are not proactive in our choices. Take decisive and immediate action. It doesn't matter if you are a genius, highly educated, uneducated, or displaced, you can't change anything or make any sort of real-life progress without taking action. Knowledge and wisdom are both useless without action. There's a huge difference between knowing and doing.

- **Connect with a passion of your heart:** Your passion will help drive you to make a difference.
- **Break it down:** Breaking passion projects down into steps makes everything doable.
- **Create a timeline:** Timely goals will help keep you motivated.
- **Support:** Surround yourself with people who believe in you.
- **Record your progress:** Collecting data will help you see where you came from and where you are going.

FROM THE ROOT TO THE FRUIT

There are over twenty-three thousand types of trees, and every type has roots. The root system of a tree usually grows between two to four times the width of the tree, establishing a foundation for growth, and is fed by the water and minerals of the soil. The better the soil is, the stronger the roots are and the healthier the tree is. You usually can't see the roots, but they determine the health of that tree. And so it goes in our lives. We are fed by our unseen values and how we water them. If we have no values to water, then our lives will bear no fruit. If we have a beautiful piece of fruit in our lives and we pull it from the source that is fed by its values, then the appearance will begin to fade and the inside will begin to rot. Bad soil or a bad environment will prevent our values from being rooted in good soil. You know people like this; don't be one of them. Root your life in good soil and water your values. In other words, ground yourself and surround yourself with strong core values. Water them to grow strong roots physically, emotionally, and spiritually. Once you identify and feed your core values, don't fall from the tree. Stay connected!

FRIENDSHIP ROLES

Studies have shown that an average person can have up to four hundred friendships over a lifetime. We have friends who do a lot more for us than we do for them. We have friends who are fun to be around but can be flaky and leave us hanging. We have friends who are awesome but gone before we know it. We have friends who make everything happen for us whether we want it or not. We have friends who will give us a shoulder to cry on and then use ours to do the same. We have friends who have been with us in our rebellious times, and we have friends who started out bright but burned up in a flash. We have friends about whom we can tell stories as they have helped shape us. We have friends whom we outgrow. We have some friends, like family, with whom we are stuck. If you are like me, your *close* friends are very few. Studies suggests that Americans' lists of close friends has shrunk to two, down from three. These are the few friends who put air under your wings and bring life to your bones. If you are anything like me, these friends are on sacred ground and held close in your innermost court. I thank God for my very special friends and for the four hundred friendships that have helped me in my journey. Be grateful, and let your friends know how much you appreciate them.

WARRIOR OR WORRIER

When we are faced with a financial crisis, health crisis, family crisis, or relational crisis, we can become soaked in a pool of worry or a pool of "glory." I will never fully understand why bad things happen to good people. What I do fully understand is that God is good all the time. On this side of heaven, we will constantly face the fear of the unknown and the results of crises. This is the time we must choose whether to be warriors or worriers. I know the results of worrying are fear, anxiety, depression, insomnia, sickness, anger, frustration, insecurity, mistrust, and impatience, just to name a few. I also know that the results of being a warrior are trust, peace, faith, security, courage, strength, patience, perseverance, and hope, just to name a few. When we encounter the giants and lions of everyday life, we have a choice of which pool to get soaked in and the results of getting wet. "As for me and my house, we will serve the Lord" (Jer. 24:15). I become a warrior when I am wet with the Word of God. I can stand up with David's words, "Whenever I am afraid, I will trust in the Lord" (Ps. 56:3). I've heard it said that "courage is just fear that has said its prayers." I invite you to soak as a warrior and not as a worrier.

FROM THE INSIDE OUT

A rose blossoms from the inside out. One of the most difficult lessons in life is learning to not be controlled by events, circumstances, and emotions. All of these things can cover us like a wet blanket. When we experience a "come to Jesus" moment, our cores are transformed to push change from the inside out. "He who believes in Me, as the Scripture said, from his innermost being will flow rivers of living water" (John 7:38). Our attitudes are rooted in our cores. Our words and actions are rooted in our attitudes. The results in our lives follow an inside-out flow, from our cores to attitudes to words to actions to results. Instead of asking, "Can God?" I will say, "God can!" A positive attitude comes from my core. Don't let depression, anxieties, and perceptions control you; believe, trust, and persevere from your innermost being as you grow closer to God.

BEING
HAPPY ON THE JOB

Happiness involves feeling good about yourself and what you are doing as a result of it. Our happiness is based on relationships and achievements. Many people will spend a majority of their lives working. When our gifts and abilities are being developed and utilized throughout our lives, we grow in confidence and strength. Here are some keys to being happy on the job:

- **See work as a gift, not a punishment:** Just changing your perceptions can make a huge difference in your attitude.
- **Pursue work that lines up with your gifts and abilities:** We must know and grow in our strengths.
- **Learn everything possible about your job:** This keeps your mind fresh and will benefit you and the job you serve.
- **Use criticism to your advantage:** Sandpaper smoothes rough edges, so let the things that rub you the wrong way smooth you out.
- **Do more than what is expected of you:** The extra mile paves new roads.

WALK BY FAITH

I spent two days watching world-class athletes compete at the Drake Relays. We had the perfect seats on the final turn as we witnessed the grimaces and determination of these competitors in their race to the finish line. The most inspiring of all was a blind man who was racing in the Paralympic 200 meter race; these athletes were preparing to compete in the Beijing 2016 Olympics. He had another world-class runner beside him with a rope between them whose job was to keep the blind athlete in his lane as he made the turns. The blind athlete gave it everything he had in running the race of his lifetime. As he ran by us, I noticed that he had sunglasses with gold metallic tape over the lenses. His faith eyes were focused on the gold at the finish line. We have an incredible presence of a savior running beside us in the race of our lives. Let us learn to rely on His tug to keep us in our lanes and to stay faith focused on the gold at the finish line. Here is an acronym to help us "walk by faith and not by sight."

- **Work:** Walking by faith means working and living life in light of eternal consequences.
- **Aim:** We must work with aim, purpose, and direction.
- **Love:** We must be anchored in love with every thought, choice, and action.
- **Kindness:** Every step we take must leave an imprint of kindness.

TARGET PRACTICE

I took my twins out target shooting with a Daisy BB rifle. While shooting, all three of us discovered that the sight on the rifle was set too low. If we aimed using that sight, we hit the bottom of the targets. We had to aim high to hit anywhere near the cans we used as targets. Isn't life a lot like that? If we set our sights too low, we don't accomplish all that we can. Sometimes we have to aim high in order to reach a desired goal. As author Bob Moawad said, "Most people don't aim too high and miss. They aim too low and hit." The only way we can reach our fullest potential is to aim high and not settle for the mediocrity of life. By aiming low, we remain in the hamster wheel of life, running and accomplishing very little. If the sight on our vision is low, we need to reset it and raise our expectations. Allow your targets to be rewarding every time you hit one. Have fun target shooting.

FEAR OR FAITH: YOUR CHOICE

Picture a train track with two tunnels ahead. One tunnel is a tunnel of fear (False Expectations Appearing Real), and the second is a tunnel of faith (Fear Ain't In This House). The walls inside each tunnel govern our thoughts and the direction our thoughts lead us. Both tunnels lead to somewhere and have significant results that impact our lives. Let's look at a few of the differences.

- Faith leads to freedom, and fear leads to bondage.
- Faith leads to mobility, and fear leads to paralysis.
- Faith leads to hope, and fear leads to despair.
- Faith leads to light at the end of the tunnel, and fear leads to darkness.

Where you drive your thoughts is your choice. I choose faith. How about you?

A PARENT'S AND COACH'S WISH

I heard a remark once that stirred a standard of behavior we can all adopt and learn from. Whether you are a parent, coach, teacher, or pastor, there is a common wish for all whom you influence. There are two things we want team members to remember every time they put on a uniform: 1) always represent the logo on the front—play hard, work hard, and be 100 percent committed to what is on your chest, and 2) honor the name on your back—be honest, build character, be respectful, and do the right thing. If we can apply these two principles to every aspect of our lives while representing our teams, jobs, schools, churches, professions, or trades, we will not only be winners; we will influence others to be winners as well.

LOG RIDE

One of my favorite rides at an amusement park is the log ride. The best part is getting wet on a hot day while experiencing the climbs, drops, and turns of a fast-moving current of water that is in complete control of your short, three-minute journey. The silent, subtle, and dangerous shift from amusement to alarm happens when we fail to exit. Life's currents have the ability to sweep us away when we are not aware of the dangers associated with the rapids that are waiting to tip us over and bang us up as we reach out to hold on for dear life. Some of the signs of drifting away are slipping back into old habits, not making amends to forgive ourselves or others for an offense, doing things that are expedient and comfortable instead of right, feeding the bark of the bad wolf instead of the cry of the good wolf, and watching relationships fall away in the wake of the current. These signs and symptoms (and others) become the root of attitude shifts that contribute to behaviors that hinder us from living to our full potential. If you find yourself drifting off course, take the nearest exit. Refocus and start living your life with purpose. Resist holding on to driftwood and take hold of God's plan for your life. "You're blessed when you stay on course, walking steadily on the road revealed by God. You're blessed when you follow his directions, doing your best to find him" (Ps. 119:1–2).

WE ARE ALL OLYMPIANS

I love the Olympics because they show the world that there are people who are living out their dreams. Whether they are athletes, coaches, trainers, or families, all are part of the vision of getting the gold medal. Life is a gold medal race in which we are all participating. Here are some disciplines that will help you carry the torch of life:

- Don't run aimlessly; set a goal for yourself and go after it.
- Don't fight like a man or woman beating the air. Make sure your fight is in line with your goals; otherwise, you will wear yourself out.
- Stay motivated; keep your track shoes on even when your feet are sore.
- Keep jumping the hurdles; if you fall, get up. The hurdle that tripped you is behind you. Every hurdle you jump is getting you closer to the finish line

STOP

The beautiful thing about brakes on a car is that we can avoid many collisions when we apply them. If we stay alert, keep our eyes on the road, and keep our hands on the wheel, we can learn when and how to use the brakes. Using them properly allows us to *stop* before major damage is incurred. As we communicate in life, we are going to enter many different intersections with people. If we can learn to apply the brakes before a collision, we can prevent a lot of damage that could dent or even total a relationship. Here are some things that could help avoid a serious collision in our relationships:

- **Stop** when you see a collision coming.
- **Talk** about things before you let your foot off the brake.
- **Options** that will avoid the wreck in communication can be discussed.
- **Practice** what you have discussed.

THE VISION, THE VENTURE, AND THE VICTORY

Have you ever set out to do something that you believed was the right thing to do and then found out that God had other plans? I know I have built my case and presented my plans before the Lord only to find God redirecting my path. "The steps of good men are directed by the Lord. He delights in each step they take" (Ps. 37:23). This has applied to me personally, my family, finances, moves, business, decisions, dating, church, and so on. I also believe the "stops" of good men are ordered by the Lord. We must be sensitive to the Holy Spirit. It is vitally important for all of us to do things God's way and not our way personally and corporately. If we insist on having our way, God may do something that we won't like in the end—He may let us do it our way. Been there, done that! We should pray every day, "Lord, I am available today for you to tell me where to go, what to do, what to say, when to say it, and when to do it." The vision is to see ahead, the venture is to take the steps in moving forward, and the victory is knowing we are being used to make a difference.

BEEP! BEEP! BEEP!

When a garbage truck backs up, you can hear the unmistakable *Beep! Beep! Beep!* This means you had better get out of the way or throw whatever garbage you have in the truck so it can take it far, far away. The average adult makes thirty-five thousand choices in a day, so it is important to recognize when we make a bad choice. The beeping sound should go off in our heads when that happens, and we should slow down to recognize that we have an opportunity to make things right. Too often, we miss the garbage truck and continue in our day, piling up garbage on the curbs of our lives. We need to take advantage of the garbage truck as it will carry away things we shouldn't have said or done. We do this by admitting and confessing the wrong choice at the time we make it. By slowing down, admitting a mistake, and correcting it, we take the stench of trash out of our lives. Holding on to garbage can contaminate a very good day, month, year, and life. Listen to the *beep* and throw away your garbage before it overtakes you.

FOCUS ALIGNS YOUR PURPOSE

Top ten list on being focused

Being focused does the following:

1) **Keeps you on target:** Taking aim keeps you moving toward your target.
2) **Increases your energy:** Energy comes from knowing where you are going and being determined to get there.
3) **Lifts you up:** Focus is like a tow rope pulling you forward.
4) **Causes you to look for a better way:** Wise choices are made when you are focused.
5) **Lets you concentrate a little harder and a little longer:** Your mind and thoughts are yoked.
6) **Allows you to make commitments, not excuses:** What you commit yourself to determines what you do.
7) **Keeps you from living in the past:** Focus dictates your future.
8) **Creates rewards, not difficulties:** You collect rewards on a focused path.
9) **Permits you to choose friends carefully:** The right friends help you stay focused.
10) **Anchors you in your strengths, not weaknesses:** When you focus on your strengths, you become stronger.

You can get over the speed bumps of the day when your focus aligns with your purpose.

FIVE LESSONS FROM A PENCIL

We all need to be constantly sharpened throughout life. We are all uniquely created with the ability to leave a mark. Through God's favor and mercy, our mistakes are erased and we are given the opportunity to correct and move forward. Never allow yourself to sink into discouragement and think your life can't change. You are significant. I read this several years ago and have not been able to credit the author. It is a simple message with profound results.

A pencil maker told a pencil five important lessons:

1) Everything you do will always leave a mark.
2) You can always correct the mistakes you make.
3) What's inside you is most important.
4) In life, you will undergo painful sharpenings which will make you a better pencil.
5) To be the best you can be, you must allow yourself to be held and guided by the hand that holds you! (Author unknown)

Like the pencil, the most important part of who you are is on the inside waiting to be sharpened and used. God wants to fulfill the purpose that you were born to accomplish. It's time to get the lead out.

HOLIDAY HARMONY

With the holiday season upon us, family dysfunctions can light up like a Christmas tree. The Thanksgiving dinners and family gatherings are often full of friction and sparks from unresolved issues. The kitchen, dining room table, and living room can be very awkward places of conversation. The reality of life is that there may never be unity. Everybody is unique and different in their opinions and perceptions. Something we can do is strive for harmony when there is no unity. Harmony is the blending of different musical notes played or sung at the same time to produce a pleasing sound. If we can learn to listen and accept the different notes in our family song, we can be part of unwrapping a gift in our family differences. A jigsaw puzzle has many unique pieces when separated. They are different shapes with diverse edges that can cut when they are exposed and separated. Many of our families are broken puzzles with fragmented pieces and edges. Harmonizing our differences will bring us together more than trying to bring unity will. Inclusion of the puzzle pieces can bring harmony within the family structure. Value, respect, and support can be restored. Let us harmonize with one another this holiday season.

NEW FILTER, NEW OIL

With the holidays fast approaching, let's do all we can to change our dirty mental filters with fresh-thinking oil as we fill the dining room and living room with our loved ones. Too often, a bad mental filter combined with dirty mental oil will cause broken relationships and rundown families. This is the perfect time to make the needed change. If you are holding someone hostage for an injustice, free them and let them go. If someone is holding you hostage for something you did, own it, apologize, and get up and out of the pothole. Grudges, guilt, judging, and umpiring keep your filter dirty, causing separation with loved ones. Change your filter (Word of God) and add new oil (Holy Spirit) to make this holiday season a moral, honest, and righteous one. "Learn to do what is right and commit yourselves to it" (Isa. 1:17). Now is the time!

ARE YOU TRAVELING OVER THE HOLIDAYS?

A traveler was preparing for a long trip. A friend asked if he was all packed, and he said, "Yup, just about. I've got my guidebook, a lamp, a mirror, a microscope, a volume of fine poetry, a package of old letters, a songbook, a sword, a hammer, a compass, a shield, a comforter, and a set of books." "But," the friend said, "you can't get all of that in one suitcase." "Sure I can," replied the traveler. "It doesn't take much room." Then he placed his Bible in the suitcase and closed the lid. The most important things we can pack on our travels are our values and integrity. The Word not only influences us, but it allows us to be influencers. Every step, every thought, and every action creates a ripple. Let us pack efficiently with purpose and intent not only this season but for every season in our lives. Blessings to you and your families as you travel this holiday season.

VERY THANKFUL

I love this time of year as we can slow down and be *very thankful* for all we have. Here are some Thanksgiving ingredients to add to our family, food, and football:

- Values that guide me and direct me from the core of my being
- Experiences that make me who I am today
- Remembering all the details of my journey
- Yoke of being next to my family, friends, and faith
- Time that I have every day to make the right choice
- Health to breathe in and enjoy the surroundings
- Attitudes that can change as I become aware of their power to live
- Nearsighted to see and observe the things that are close to me
- Kindness that others have shown me
- Forgiveness that I have given to others and others have given me
- Understanding that opens the window of my eyes and heart
- Laughter that is medicine for my soul

SPREAD THE LOVE, NOT THE OFFENSE

One of the greatest tools of wisdom is recorded in Proverbs 17:9: "He who covers over an offense spreads love, but whoever spreads the matter separates close friends." One of Noah's sons found him in an embarrassing spot after a tough night. The son went out to spread the offense (gossip), but his two brothers shut him up and covered their dad's shame with an act of love. The consequence of spreading someone's mistake is never good. The immediate gratification can make us feel good or look better as we beat our chests and wave our flags. The reality is that by repeating the matter we are distancing ourselves from our close friends. Once we learn to look at others as being more important than we are, we see them differently. Rather than looking down on people, we look up at them. Are we spreading love, or are we spreading the offense?

BEING THANKFUL ELIMINATES BEING SELFISH

A thankful heart is the victory over selfish desires. The Garden of Eden was filled with every food and accommodation needed to satisfy Adam and Eve, and thankfulness was at the core of their being. They were asked to stay away from one thing, the forbidden fruit. When temptation overcomes thankfulness, we are derailed from the direction we were created for. Oprah Winfrey said, "Be thankful for what you have; you'll end up having more. If you concentrate on what you don't have, you will never, ever have enough." When we focus on things that we don't have or on situations that compromise our values, our minds become darkened and we take for granted life, family, sunshine, flowers, salvation, and God. The best way to turn your life around is to be thankful for what you have and take nothing for granted. The fall of humankind began with the chase for something that was forbidden. Let's be addicted to thankfulness rather than to something that is bad for us. The choice is ours. Am I thankful for what I have, or am I driven to get what I don't have? Choose with me an attitude of gratitude and be thankful for a God that loves us.

MAKE IT A GREAT DAY

We have the ability to make it a great day every time we wake up in the morning. Our reaction to events and circumstances is in our control. Here are a few guidelines that could turn your day around as soon as you open your eyes. These are three things that we can wrap our heads, hearts, and arms around.

- **Head:** Today I will commit to learning something new. There is something for me to learn.
- **Heart:** Today I will commit to a passion in my heart. There is something for me to feel.
- **Hands:** Today I will commit to doing something that makes a difference. There is something I can do that will benefit somebody else.

I will have a great day if I have something to know, something to feel, and something to do.

LOVING GOD MORE TODAY THAN YESTERDAY

I would like to invite you to join me on a personal mission of loving God and people more today than yesterday. This comes from the words of Jesus recorded in Mark 12:30–31: "Love the Lord your God with all your heart and with all your soul and with all your mind and with all your strength." I want you to picture a heart with a cross in the center. The heart has four chambers, and the cross forms the divisions between the chambers. Each of these words—heart (your innermost part), soul (your nature and being), mind (your ability to think, reason, perceive, feel, and remember), and strength (your ability to resist force and being broken)—represent a chamber in the heart of God. When one of the chambers is not working, the heart stops. It takes a daily effort in our journey with God to love Him with every part of His heart for us. When we love God with our hearts, souls, minds, and strength and glue together what we think, what we know, what we say, and what we do, we will live our lives with purpose.

LOVING PEOPLE MORE TODAY THAN YESTERDAY

"Love the Lord your God with all your heart and with all your soul and with all your mind and with all your strength. The second is this: 'Love your neighbor as yourself'" (Mark 12:30–31). Yesterday we learned about loving God. Today we are focusing on loving others as we love ourselves. The message in Jesus's words (love your neighbor) does not merely mean one who lives nearby but anyone we meet. If I lift my eyes up and extend my arms, I am replicating a cross: up loving God and out loving people. If I am connected to the cross vertically with my heart, soul, mind, and strength and I am connected horizontally, there is a ripple effect of God's love for me and others. The greatest difference we can make in this life is to love God and people more today than yesterday.

THANKFULNESS BURIES THE KILLER CS

Have you ever noticed that some people seem to be able to maintain an attitude of gratitude regardless of what's happening around them? They see the good in difficult people, they see the opportunity in a challenging situation, and they appreciate what they have, even in the face of loss. These people have the ability to bury the killer Cs that can overtake us and cripple us. The killer Cs are *criticizing, complaining*, and *controlling*. Here are some benefits of eliminating the Cs with thankfulness:

- Thankfulness buries the *critic* that judges and finds fault. When we are grateful, our eyes and thoughts are looking up to someone rather than looking down on someone.
- Thankfulness buries the *complainer* that is never satisfied. When we are grateful, our focus is on appreciating what we have instead of on what we don't have.
- Thankfulness buries the *controller* that has a tight hold on everything. When we are grateful, our grip on the steering wheel loosens.

THANKFULNESS:
THE PERFECT CURE FOR VENOM

Thanksgiving week is my favorite week of the year as we purpose in our hearts to be grateful. We have all been affected throughout life with poisonous venom. The poisonous venom of a snake bite causes blood to clot and can be fatal if not removed quickly. The venom of pain and hurt in relationships can cause the same fatal clots between people if not dealt with. The perfect cure for venom is a grateful heart. If we can learn to fill our veins with gratitude, there is no room for poison because we always become a better person through our trials and adversities. Forgive, forget, and move forward. Studies have proved that gratitude promotes psychological well-being, healthy living, and prosocial or moral behavior. Studies have also shown that there are higher levels of positive mood and lower levels of negative mood in people who practice thankfulness. "So let the peace that comes from Christ control your thoughts. And be grateful" (Col. 3:15).

LOVING FROM A DISTANCE

One of the most difficult things we experience in life is having to love from a distance. There are times that we can't speak to or be physically present to walk beside the ones we love. So many things can be barriers to doing what we feel, want, and desire to do.

> When your heart is breaking for someone who is broken, but your words can't reach them and your love can't save them, ask the angels to go where you cannot. To whisper into their heart what their ears can't hear: "We will not give up in you. Don't give up on yourself." (Sandra Kring)

Prayer is a wonderful coping tool to use in times of stress. It allows us to include God in the frustration we have from not being able to respond. Mary, the mother of Jesus, had the most difficult example of loving from a distance as she watched her son suffer a brutal beating and death while hanging on a cross. There is nothing harder in life than not being able to do anything. Our only light at the end of this dark tunnel is to know and believe in something beyond. Pray for God's presence when yours is not possible.

GETTING OUT OF PARK

Picture life as an automobile. Hope scrapes the mud off the windshield so we can see something that is beyond our circumstances. Faith is the gas pedal that we press to get out and beyond the park position or ditch. Love is the fuel in the tank that is the source for our movement. Without fuel, we can't go anywhere. It takes love to get us to have enough faith to move beyond ourselves. In our journey through life, we are always in one of three seasons on the road we travel. We are either driving into a storm, driving in a storm, or driving out of a storm. The common thread to understanding all three seasons is that we are always surrounded by storms. Love is the fuel, faith is the accelerator, and hope is a clear enough windshield to provide direction.

THE THREE RS

Every one of us goes through life being offended or offending someone else. Unattended anger is poison in the heart. Every time I replay an injustice done to me or an injustice I have done to others, I am letting toxin exude from my pores. There is tremendous power in an apology. It's like an antiseptic that cools, heals, and restores wounds. As a result, relationships become stronger and hearts become mended. The three Rs are tools to help us.

- **Regret** starts in the head, where we sincerely process things.
- **Responsibility** begins in the heart, where an honest response is taken deeply.
- **Resolve** is when the commitment is put into place with integrity.

Our thoughts (head), words (heart), and action (hands) determine the power of an apology. Let today be the beginning of a new tomorrow. The Rs have it!

DO I HAVE A SONG IN MY HEART?

Chirpie's owner was vacuuming his cage one day when the phone rang. As she reached over to answer the phone, *ssschloop!* Chirpie got sucked in. The bird owner gasped, put down the phone, turned off the vacuum, and opened the bag. There was Chirpie—still alive but stunned. She grabbed him and raced to the bathroom, turned on the faucet, and held Chirpie under the running water. As Chirpie was soaked and shivering, the owner reached for the hair dryer and blasted the pet with hot air. Poor Chirpie never knew what hit him. Chirpie doesn't sing much anymore; he just sits and stares. Sucked in, washed up, and blown over, Chirpie lost his song. Scriptures tell us we are created to worship just like Chirpie. The traumas of life can stun us, and we can lose our voice. Jesus faced the worst trauma ever known to humankind, His brutal death. "Now my soul is troubled, and what shall I say? 'Father, save me from this hour'? No, it was for this very reason I came to this hour. Father, glorify your name!" (John 12:27–28). No matter how bad it gets, *keep singing!*

THINGS MUST WORK
IN ME BEFORE THEY WORK FOR ME

Have you ever tried to do something because it worked for other people and you wanted their results? Thousands of diets are designed and produced to curb your appetite. Thousands of exercise routines are guaranteed to get you in shape, and thousands of products are available to help you quit smoking, drinking, and other addictive habits. Billions of dollars are spent on products advertised in infomercials and commercials to get you to change into something new and different. *Breaking News:* Things must first work *in* me before they work *for* me! Let's talk about God: "When you received the Word of God, which you heard from us, you accepted it not as a human word, but as it actually is, the Word of God, which is indeed at work *in* you who believe" (1 Thess. 2:13, emphasis added). Knowing God is not about joining a religion or a church so you can be part of something. It is about an *inward* change of your heart. When we believe, we chase the heart of God. The results are working *in* us before they work *for* us. If we want His blessings, we must meet His conditions.

DISTRACTIONS

One day, I was T-boned while driving. I had a green light and was traveling through an intersection. Another vehicle turned into me, causing my car to spin and collide with another car. I was pinned such that first responders had to saw the car to free me. I had non-life-threatening injuries and was very fortunate to survive. I found out later that the young person who hit me had been texting and not paying attention. Texting and driving has become an uncontrollable epidemic. People are becoming addicted to their phones and feel the need to respond immediately to any notifications on their devices. According to a study by the Virginia Tech Transportation Institute, sending or receiving a text takes a driver's eyes off the road for an average of 4.6 seconds, the equivalent of driving blind at fifty-five miles per hour for the length of an entire football field. With attention distracted, it is like driving blindfolded for those few seconds. The results can be and often are fatal. *TeenDriving.AAA.com* reports that six out of ten teen crashes involve driver distraction. We must train and teach our kids, family members, friends, and associates that no text or call is worth the few seconds of distraction that could end in life-changing consequences.

THERE IS VALUE IN A TEA BAG

Tea comes in many flavors and assortments. Tea bags come alive and produce flavor after being exposed to heat. When hot water is added to the tea bag, the tea bag opens and adds an essence and taste to its environment. Hot water in the world we live in can do the same for us. Our inner being and core can come alive under the heat that surrounds us. "Consider it pure joy, my brothers and sisters, whenever you face trials of many kinds, because you know that the testing of your faith produces perseverance. Let perseverance finish its work so that you may be mature and complete, not lacking anything" (James 1:2–4). If we can learn to allow the heat that surrounds us to begin and complete a work within us, we can become mature and complete. We must learn to continue and not give up when the heat is on. We must persevere through all the hot water that life brings. Let the heat bring out the best in you.

DIFFICULT TRADITIONS

Are you looking ahead at a mountain of traditions that are overwhelming and unbearable? Is it impossible to put on a game face when everyone around you is joyful? Has the pain of sorrow and loss blurred any vision of seeing ahead? So many things knock the wind out of us—death of a loved one, death of a pet, divorce, a looming relational end, diagnosis of terminal disease, financial hardship, and so on. Here is a list of ten tools that can help you navigate the difficult weeks ahead:

- "No" is a complete sentence. Use it. Well-meaning people will try to fill your schedule.
- It's okay to take a year off. One thing is for certain—next year will roll around quickly.
- Decide what you don't want or like and replace it with comfort.
- Have an exit strategy to get off the holiday highway.
- Tell people what you are comfortable with.
- Create your own personal traditions.
- Take on a holiday project that helps someone.
- Close your eyes, remember something that made you happy, and smile back.
- Maybe something was left undone. Complete the project or deed in honor of your loss.
- Plan for something in January.

Surround yourself with people you trust and add new tools to your toolbox of survival. You are loved!

THE WINDSHIELD IS BIGGER THAN THE REARVIEW MIRROR

We can use the windshield as an example of the journey of life. It is much bigger than the rearview mirror. The rearview mirror reflects where I have been, while the windshield shows where I am going. Too often I focus on what is behind me rather than what is ahead of me. If my eyes are focused on the rearview mirror, I am in danger of getting into a crash. The past crashes are what have gotten me to the present point in my journey, allowing me to see through the much bigger windshield. One of the keys to victory in life is to use what is behind me to focus on what is ahead me. I can't move forward if my eyes are focused on the past. I must look straight ahead, using the things behind me as experiences to fuel where I am going.

DEBT AND BORROWING

Financial debt and borrowing can dig us a six-foot-deep hole if we are not careful. Financial difficulties are the number-one cause for relationship failure. All through scripture, debt is discussed in a negative tone. The main reason for this is that debt makes us a servant to someone other than God. When we borrow, we become a servant to a bank, a business, a family member, a friend—whomever we borrowed from. When we borrow, the lender puts conditions on the loan, stating what we can and cannot do. This makes us servants to them. "The rich rule over the poor, and the borrower is servant to the lender" (Prov. 22:7). If we do borrow, we must pay back all the debt. The circumstances don't matter, even if they're beyond our control. We should only borrow if we have a guarantee. If everything goes as we expect, we'll be able to pay the loans back. If things go wrong, as they often do, we may be left in debt. Try to avoid long-term debt. Scriptures guide us to pay everything off within seven years. If you can qualify for a fifteen-year mortgage, try to pay it off in seven years.

CUTTING THE
ANCHORS OF GUILT AND SHAME

Being ashamed of who we are or feeling guilty for what we have done or what has been done to us are two anchors in life that immobilize us and keep us from moving forward. Even when we think we have succeeded in hiding our feelings, thoughts, and attitudes, our guilt and shame come out in other ways. Some of these behaviors can include compulsive behaviors, sexual addictions, overeating, chemical and alcohol abuse, and depression. Here are a few tools to help you get rid of the guilt and shame:

- Stop beating yourself up. You are not a whack-a-mole.
- Treat yourself to fun and innovative things.
- Open up to fresh thinking and get rid of the negative self-talk.
- Power up for the future by releasing the anchor.

IF ONLY WE KNEW

We don't know when it will happen
When our kin receive the call
Our families are shattered
The effects felt by all
Our loss has many faces
Some by nature, some by man
One thing is for certain
We need to hold each other's hands
What can we do
When tragedy comes our way
Will we help someone out
Or will we turn and run away
The best thing we can do
Is to offer our lives for those in need
And to know we make a difference … for someone else
Many hearts need our attention
As the pain's too much to bear
One thing is certain
There's lots of work for those who care
That's why love is so important
To help us in our loss
Someone there right beside us
To help us carry our cross

PRINCIPLES, PRIORITIES, AND PRACTICES

Life is like music. You have high notes, and you have low notes. Put the right notes together and you have a chord. Life is in harmony when we play the right notes. These three notes (principles, priorities, and practices) are a harmonizing chord that resonates direction and purpose in life. Principles are a core foundation for our beliefs, our behavior, and our reasoning. Priorities are the things that are regarded or treated as more important than others. Practices are the actual applications of the principles and priorities. Character and integrity are the result of these three chords being played. People will pick up on the harmony and tune you live and play by when these three are in unison playing your life chord. So the journey goes from our hearts to our heads to our hands. If we can play these three notes at the same time, we will make beautiful music.

HOPE, FAITH, LOVE

The apostle Paul used these three words to help define and direct our futures. Too often we get stuck without the ability to move forward. This could lead to depression, which is the state of not being able to construct any future. The perceived result is no light at the end of a dark tunnel. Hope brings light at the end of that dark tunnel, faith is the belief that you can walk toward the light, and love is the fuel to move. Here are three acronyms to help understand the power of combining three actions to help us attain things we can't see:

Hope Opens People's Eyes
Fear Ain't In This House
Living Outside Vulnerable Experiences

Hope opens up new windows, faith allows us to move toward the things we hope for, and love makes it all happen.

THE WAVES OF HOLIDAY GRIEF

The holidays are always a difficult time when we are constantly experiencing and facing the loss of a loved one. The sights, smells, and sounds of the season can trigger waves of emotion that crash in on us. These waves will come out of nowhere when we least expect them, with power and the potential to wash us away as we tumble bruised and battered onto the shore. We must accept and understand that these waves are going to come with a heightened surge of power this time of year. Rather than standing helpless in the path of the wave, there are three things we can do to keep us from drowning using the waves as a metaphor for handing the surge of emotions.

1) Take a defensive posture with your body turned sideways. Hold on to your forearm and lean into the surge with your shoulder and head at impact. This will keep you from being blindsided.
2) When the surge is at the point of impact, duck below and allow the major force of the wave to crash above you.
3) Turn around with your arms pointed toward the shoreline. At the crest of the wave, duck your head and allow your body to ride the wave until it subsides.

The emotional waves will come, and we can't avoid their surge. We can only try different ways to defend ourselves. Know that you are loved and are not alone as you face the waves of holiday grief.

WHAT'S ON MY TREE?

Christmas is a time for hanging ornaments on trees. Let's imagine that you and I are Christmas trees. If I am to be a tree of life, the scriptures are pretty clear about what ornaments God wants hanging on me. "'And you shall love the LORD your God with all your heart, with all your soul, with all your mind, and with all your strength.' This is the first commandment. And the second, like it, is this: 'You shall love your neighbor as yourself.' There is no other commandment greater than these" (Mark 12:30–31). These four ornaments (heart, soul, mind, and strength)—all baked in love—need to hang on my tree. The greatest gift we can give to anyone is a pure heart, a clean soul, a sound mind, and strength to do the right thing. Anytime our heads, hearts, and hands are working together in unison, we become God's ornament. Be a gift to those around you.

WHERE IS THE LINE TO SEE JESUS?

As the hectic holiday season of Christmas is upon our nation, where is the line to see Jesus? People are lining up to buy merchandise, to see movies, to eat at restaurants, to see football games, to register for next-semester classes, to experience rides at adventure parks, to mail packages at the post office, and so on. Our lives are busier than ever. We are a people carving out time for God in our busy lives when we should be carving out our lives from our time with God. A still, small voice is crying out for all of us to line up to experience God. The innermost sanctuary of God's presence is where we need to be. It's where we must be to survive the storms, floods, hurricanes, and satanic terrorist attacks on our minds, souls, and bodies. There is a war around us. Hiding in the presence of God is what must capture our hearts. We are a people who must transition from being worldly driven to presence driven. It's time to line up to see Jesus.

WAYS TO COPE WITH GRIEF

You can't go over, under, or around grief; you must go through it, in your own way and at your own pace. There is no cookie-cutter process or organized guidelines for people to follow. Everyone is unique and different in navigating their personal journey through the pain of loss. Here are a few things that might help you in coping with grief:

- Talk with friends and family members who will listen. Sometimes, our inner circle of people can be a help in coping with grief. They know us the best and can offer genuine support in times of need.
- Get involved in your church and seek the fellowship of other believers. Faith-based support can give you strength to walk through this difficult time.
- Get involved with a support group for those going through similar losses. Support groups provide a comfort in your loss as those who attend are suffering the same kind of pain.
- Set up a counseling appointment. Professional help can be very valuable in moving forward. Trained professionals can offer guidance and direction in your journey.

AVOID THE HOLIDAY CRASH

You may not always look where you are going, but you will always end up going where you are looking. Have you ever secretly desired someone else's property, spouse, job, or house? Once we take our eyes off the road, we can lose control and spin into a ditch. Along with holiday cheer comes icy roads and black ice. The grass isn't greener on the other side of the fence. Before we start playing in someone else's yard, we need to fertilize our own. Before we park in someone else's garage, we need to clean ours out and make room for what we have. The garage is our mind, and our eyes are the garage door opener. Keep your eyes up and focused, and you will avoid the holiday crash. "My eyes are fixed on you, Sovereign LORD; in you I take refuge. Keep me safe from the traps set before me" (Ps. 147:8–9).

HOLIDAY SURVIVAL KIT

For most people the holidays are a joyful time of family, friends, food, and fun. We are barraged with suggestive marketing to buy, buy, and buy more. At a time when stores are competing for our money, there are many who are sad, lonely, and depressed. The passing of a loved one, the constant rewind of broken relationships, the loss of income, and the passing of a pet are just a few holes that are magnified during the holidays. Here are some tools to help make this a holy Christmas season:

- Faith gives us the ability to rise above circumstances so we can begin to see a much higher purpose.
- Adopt and commit to traditions that benefit others.
- Welcome, accept, and invite a divine spiritual presence of Jesus and others.
- Put on your comforter (made up of collected comfort resource squares that have warmed you throughout your lifetime) for yourself and others.

HOLIDAY CHOICE TEST

The average person makes thirty-five thousand choices a day. The choices we make today have an impact on the decisions we will be making tomorrow. They establish a pattern and a foundation for our lives. Consider shopping. The average American supermarket carries around thirty-six thousand items for sale. Crest offers thirty-six variations of its toothpaste in the choice of size, shape, and flavor. Revlon has 158 different colors of lipstick, and there are 200 new magazines that hit the market each year. As we are inundated with marketing telling us to spend and buy, here are a few tips to pass the choice test:

- Is my choice in agreement with my core values?
- Is my choice made with integrity instead of something I am hiding?
- By making this choice, will it help me be a better person?
- Will my choice become or feed an addiction?
- Will my choice benefit others?

WHO'S THAT KNOCKING AT MY DOOR?

Christmas and the New Year are a time when we invite a lot of people into our houses. We never know who is going to come knocking. "Behold, I stand at the door and knock. If anyone hears My voice and opens the door, I will come in" (Rev. 3:20). What if Jesus knocked on my door? Would I invite Him in? What do you think would happen when He crossed over the threshold? Joshua challenged his family and friends, saying, "But if you refuse to serve the LORD, then choose today whom you will serve. Would you prefer the gods your ancestors served beyond the Euphrates? Or will it be the gods of the Amorites in whose land you now live? But as for me and my house, we will serve the LORD" (Joshua 24:15). Next we will look at some of the results of a godly remodel.

HOLIDAY COMFORTER

Take a few moments and think about some things that bring you comfort, hope, and encouragement through good times and difficult times. Identify one per square in the quilt below.

Use this quilt as a comforter to pull over you at night, as a pillowcase to rest your head and thoughts on, and as a blanket to wrap around yourself and others during the day to stay warm.

R&R FOR THE HOLIDAYS

Stress, anxieties, and depression are very common during the holiday season which can take the air out of and deflate the "Merry" associated with Christmas. Some behaviors could lead to something we will regret. Some of us will spend money we don't have. Others can binge on food and caffeine. And still others can abuse alcohol. In fact, the American Psychological Association (APA) found that nearly half of all women in the United States experience heightened stress during the holidays, which puts their health at risk. The APA also learned that during this time, 41 percent of women misuse food and 28 percent misuse alcohol. For men, the misuse of alcohol is much higher. Here are some survival tips:

- Slow down and rest throughout your day. Add some stress-busting minutes that you can commit to. Create a place or space that you can escape to.
- When you wake, think happy thoughts and allow those thoughts to give you a different perception of your day.
- Prepare a nice to-do list for "others" and a nice to-do list for "self."
- Set up some eating and drinking boundaries and commit to them throughout your day.
- Allow an attitude of gratitude to help you in working with others and yourself.

UNWRAPPING YOUR "PRESENCE"

The greatest gift we can give does not come in a box. It comes from our hearts.

> Love is slow to suspect but quick to trust; slow to condemn but quick to justify; slow to offend but quick to defend; slow to expose but quick to shield; slow to reprimand but quick to empathize; slow to belittle but quick to appreciate; slow to demand but quick to give; slow to provoke but quick to help; slow to resent but quick to forgive. (The Word For You Today)

The scriptures give great guidelines on how to turn a holiday season into a lifestyle of learning to love.

- **Love believes all things:** Love teaches me to look beyond the hurt that I am in with someone I care about.
- **Love brings hope:** Love teaches me to see the potential in people and not the mud they are stuck in.
- **Love endures:** Love teaches me to throw an anchor into stormy waters. (1 Corin. 13)

A MAMA'S EYES

Mary and Joseph were traveling when it came time for the baby to be born. There were no rooms available; every hotel was packed. Little did they know that the decision they made had been decided many years before. "Away in a manger, no crib for a bed, the little Lord Jesus laid down his sweet head. The stars in the sky looked down where he lay. The little Lord Jesus asleep in the hay." As Mary looked down and held her son, do you think she realized that those little fingers were the same ones that had formed the mountains and scooped out the oceans? Do you think she realized after she counted His toes that they were the same ones that walked on streets of gold and would soon walk on water? Do you think she realized that those little lips spoke the world into existence and would soon be the living breath of God? Do you think she realized that when she kissed her baby she was kissing the face of God? Do you think she realized that as Jesus opened His eyes He would open the eyes of all who would catch His gaze? Thank you, Mary, and all the moms who birth life into existence through the life of this little baby boy. Happy birthday, Jesus!

MERRY
POSITIVE CHRISTMAS

We are hardwired with a negative bias, which causes us to notice negative events more than positive ones. Let's cultivate a positive Christmas by incorporating positivity into our emotions, our spirits, and our actions. For every negative emotional experience, seek three positive emotional experiences to uplift you. Peter Drucker said, "The best way to predict your future is to create it." Positivity creates a great future. Be encouraged and have a great Christmas.

- Majestic
- Enthusiasm
- Radiant
- Responsible
- Youthful
- Caring
- Happiness
- Reflective
- Inspirational
- Simple
- Thankful
- Motivational
- Acceptance
- Special

A YEAR
OF SIGNIFICANCE

I recently witnessed a sunrise while flying above storm clouds that were hovering over the land below. I realized then that God had bigger plans for me that were above the circumstances of life. With the New Year approaching, most of us desire to make it a significant year. The best way we can do that is to be drawn, driven, directed, and dedicated to the path that is laid out for us. "Along unfamiliar paths I will guide them; I will turn the darkness into light before them and make the rough places smooth. These are the things I will do; I will not forsake them" (Isa. 42:16).

- I must be **drawn:** "Draw near to God and He will draw near to me" (James 4:8).
- I must be **driven:** "We never give up. Our bodies are gradually dying, but we ourselves are being made stronger each day" (2 Corin. 4:16).
- I must be **directed:** "Your word is a lamp for my feet, a light on my path" (Ps. 119:105).
- I must be **dedicated:** "And whatever you do or say, do it as a representative of the Lord Jesus, giving thanks through him to God the Father" (Col. 3:17).

Let's make this a year of significance and accomplish great things. "The LORD will work out his plans for my life—for your faithful love, O LORD, endures forever" (Ps. 138:8).

FORMULA FOR A STRONG YEAR—PART ONE

I want to share a formula (85 percent, 10 percent, 5 percent) to help structure your new year. Growing up, I played a lot of sports. One of the things my dad always encouraged me to do was to explore and find something I was good at, something I enjoyed, and something I had potential to grow in and improve on. Finding your strengths is a soul-searching journey. At the young age of eleven, I tried boxing. In my tenth fight, I woke up in my dad's arms with water and a cold compress on my head. I was zero and ten with every fight ending on my back. My dad whispered in my ear, "It's time to find a new sport." I continued to find my passion in sports and pursued football, baseball, basketball, soccer, and golf. Golf eventually took over, and I played through high school and college. What I learned about my behavior and human behavior in general is that when we find our strengths, we need to focus on them. Too often while growing up, I was told to focus on my weaknesses. Throughout my life, I have come to know the power of the mind. Whatever we focus on is what we develop. If we focus on our strengths, we become stronger. If we focus on weaknesses, we become weaker. Here is a formula to adopt once you have identified your strengths. Focus 85 percent of your thoughts and energy on your strengths, 10 percent on something new to learn, and 5 percent on your weaknesses.

FORMULA FOR A STRONG YEAR—PART TWO

Focus 85 percent of your thoughts and energy on your strengths, 10 percent on something new to learn, and 5 percent on your weaknesses. I was taught as a young athlete to focus on my weaknesses, but I found that doing so wasn't allowing me to get any better. Athletes in a team sport grow and excel when they find their right positions. Once that spot is determined and accepted, a focus to become the best is encouraged. I was challenged to write a mission statement in college, and I came up with "Helping people get to a better place." I began to focus 85 percent of my time on developing this strength, 10 percent on learning new ways to develop my mission, and 5 percent on my weaknesses. At age sixty, I can tell you that everything I have ever done in my life journey has set me up for tomorrow. When we know what we want, who we are, and where we are going, life becomes an adventure of growth and opportunity; which are the results of focusing on your strengths. I encourage you to identify your strengths and work to improve them. Practice, explore, and implement your strengths in everything you do. Allow your physical, emotional, and spiritual being to grow and develop in your strengths. The weeks, months, and years ahead will follow you.

STEPPING INTO A NEW SEASON

Life is full of change, just as the four seasons that are based on the rotation of the earth as it orbits the sun are. The temperatures of our personal seasons can be as cold as the winter when we experience the separation of warmth from family and friends. This could be a time when the nighttime seems as if it will never end, the long nights when the tears seem like they will never stop flowing. The morning comes, the tears cease, and the joy returns to your spirit as a new season brings springtime weather and the budding of new life, hope, and purpose. The summer season comes with the heat that helps circulate our being, and we see the fruit of our labor and love. Then comes the fall season, when everything becomes dormant and either dies or goes into seclusion and hibernation for the winter. Our lives will change, and we will enter and exit many seasons. God doesn't measure seasons with clocks and calendars but through truth and revelation. Every season we go through has a purpose in maturing and completing us. There are some things to know and learn about seasons as we step in and out of them. They bring new **changes**, new **challenges**, and new **champions**. We are all entering a season, in the middle of a season, or coming out of a season. Keep stepping and you will become a weathered champion.

LET THE FUTURE BEGIN

I lived in the desert for forty-seven years before moving to the Midwest. I had never experienced four seasons nor the possible extremes of a winter. The springtime is incredible as flowers, vegetables, trees, birds, and smells fill the atmosphere. It is a season of new birth and life. It almost makes the winter survivable—*not!* Spring is the beginning of so many things. The sun shines and brings warmth and life. The sad part is that it lasts only for a season. After a few months, summer comes and goes, and then fall approaches. What was once full of beauty and life turns dormant and in many cases dies. The beauty of God's season is that it never ends. When we open ourselves to the beauty of God's Son, His warmth and life bring us eternal spring as our lives are transformed for His glory. In April of 1977, I opened my heart to the warmth of God's eternal season. Accepting Christ and allowing His presence to blossom in me has turned a onetime cycle of ending seasons into an eternal season of growth and fruit. If you have not opened yourself up to the Son who brings eternal warmth and life, I encourage you to. Simply say yes to the four seasons of Christ—His birth, life, death, and resurrection. These four seasons will let your eternal future begin.

THE POWER OF BEING CONTENT

As the New Year approaches, one of the things we can learn is the power of being content. Contentment isn't something at the end of a journey. It is something to learn and practice along the journey. Rather than being tripped and suffocated by adversity and hardships, we can learn to stand and breathe under pressure. Contentment is the ability to enjoy life at every detour. Here are a few tools to help with cultivating contentment:

- **Want it:** Simplifying your life will take the pressure off wanting things you don't have. The key is wanting what you have.
- **Choose it:** "Contentment makes poor men rich, and discontent makes rich men poor" (Benjamin Franklin).
- **Speak it:** If I can learn to say, "I have enough" and "I am grateful for what I have," it will help me see, smell, and enjoy the things around me.
- **Live it:** Let your lifestyle follow your desire, your choice, and your voice.

CONCLUSION

The collection of 365 daily inspirational readings in *Tools for Life* is intended to bring knowledge, insight, encouragement, motivation, and comfort. The stories have come from a lifetime of experience of helping people get to a better place physically, spiritually, and emotionally. Dr. Coyle's writings are focused on giving his readers tools to help by establishing core values and morals along with providing faith principles. The readings have random themes, with some themes centered on holidays. *Tools for Life* can be used year after year by families and friends to provide guidance and direction while navigating the day-to-day challenges of life. You are encouraged to highlight and share certain themes that have touched and inspired you. These tools are meant to be shared and used by you and others in making a difference in the world we live in. The design and purpose of the book are to give you tools to put in your life toolbox. The theme of each story is unique and provides a new way to view and experience different circumstances and events that follow us throughout our lives.